THE
FAR
SHORE

INDIE GAMES, SUPERBROTHERS, AND THE MAKING OF *JETT*

ADAM HAMMOND

COACH HOUSE BOOKS, TORONTO

first edition

Published with the generous assistance of the Canada Council for the Arts and the Ontario Arts Council. Coach House Books also acknowledges the support of the Government of Canada through the Canada Book Fund and the Government of Ontario through the Ontario Book Publishing Tax Credit.

LIBRARY AND ARCHIVES CANADA CATALOGUING IN PUBLICATION

Title: The far shore : indie games, Superbrothers, and the making of JETT / Adam Hammond.
Names: Hammond, Adam, author.
Identifiers: Canadiana (print) 20210334525 | Canadiana (ebook) 20210334576 | ISBN 9781552454206 (softcover) | ISBN 9781770566682 (EPUB) | ISBN 9781770566699 (PDF)
Subjects: LCSH: Superbrothers (Firm) | LCSH: Video games. | LCSH: Video games industry. | LCSH: Video games—Authorship. | LCSH: Video games—Design.
Classification: LCC GV1469.37 .H35 2021 | DDC 794.8/5—dc23

The Far Shore: Indie Games, Superbrothers, and the Making of JETT is available as an ebook: ISBN 978 1 77056 668 2 (EPUB), ISBN 978 1 77056 669 9 (PDF)

Purchase of the print version of this book entitles you to a free digital copy. To claim your ebook of this title, please email sales@chbooks.com with proof of purchase. (Coach House Books reserves the right to terminate the free digital download offer at any time.)

TABLE OF CONTENTS

PROLOGUE

It was late October 2013, I was in Montreal, and I was feeling famous.

Satisfaction is a dangerous feeling, but as I walked from the train station to my swanky hotel, I let it wash over me. I was teaching a popular course, 'The Digital Text,' at the best school in the country. This course had led to a book contract. The day before, I'd been a featured panelist on an international radio broadcast. I was in Montreal on an all-expense-paid trip to give a lecture about a videogame. The day after that, I would travel deep into the woods of Quebec to meet a reclusive and mysterious genius, the creator of the videogame I was lecturing on, and the subject of that contracted book.

I took this feeling into my hotel in Montreal, which was indeed almost impossibly swanky. I told them my name, the person behind the desk said I was all paid up and led me around the corner to my room – not up a flight of stairs, not into an elevator, for the room, swankily, was right there. Perhaps the swankiest part of this room was the bathroom, which was wall-to-wall with mirrors. Perfectly clean, immaculately reflective, bevel-edged mirrors that surrounded me on every side, telescoping mirrors on trestles that let you get very close to whatever body part you wanted to look at. I had never been in a room with so many mirrors. And because I had never been in a room with so many mirrors, I saw something I had never seen before. It was on the back of my head: a corona of wispy brown hair barely concealing the scalp beneath it. In its centre, no larger than a toonie, was a small but definite bald spot.

As it happened, I had been thinking a lot about bald spots around that time, though in a completely different way. Two of the people I'd written my dissertation about, the English writer Virginia Woolf and the Russian literary theorist Mikhail Bakhtin, had interesting things to say about the part of my head that, I now saw for the first time, was mostly hair-free.

In *A Room of One's Own*, Woolf writes about a 'spot the size of a shilling at the back of the head which one can never see for oneself.' Her argument is that men will never understand themselves unless women are given the chance to describe that small spot to them – that we need others to help us understand the things about ourselves that we're blind to, that the perspective of any one person is always necessarily limited, and so silencing half the population is a grave mistake.

Bakhtin says something very similar in his essay 'Art and Answerability':

> I shall always see and know something that he, from his place outside and over against me, cannot see himself: parts of his body that are inaccessible to his own gaze [...] the world behind his back, and a whole series of objects and relations, which in any of our mutual relations are accessible to me but not to him.

This is the foundation of Bakhtin's ethics: if there are things I cannot see for myself, then I need other people, and I should be good to them so that they will be honest with me.

I was planning an article about the curious fact that these two brilliant thinkers, neither of whom was aware of the other in their lifetime, had written about such similar things in such similar ways at around the same time. But standing in the swanky bathroom, the intellectual appeal of baldness vanished. I thought instead that it was incredible that the one place you can't see for yourself in a normal reflecting surface, like a mirror or a puddle or a pond, is the place that goes bald, as if all the other patches of hair stay put only because they know they're being watched. (I also thought about my clearly unethical girlfriend and other friends who had been staring at this bald spot, probably for years, without telling me about it.)

The symbolic consequences of my discovery began to hit me in waves. I had gotten used to thinking of myself as a kind of youthful renegade. With 'The Digital Text,' I was teaching a new kind of course, breathing new life into an old subject. I was on my way to investigate a totally new cultural phenomenon, indie videogames – an art form without a long history, without much of a critical tradition, mostly without rules. All this youthful energy was sucked into my newly discovered bald spot as if into a black hole.

Maybe indie games weren't some bold, new, vital burst of energy in the videogame world, but just a marker of the medium's encroaching middle age. Born in the sixties, videogames had been dismissed since then as childish and adolescent: trivial, violent, crude, stupid. The new arty subgenre of independently produced videogames that I was here to investigate was something different: without the need to please huge audiences, the small teams who made them were free to be weird, angry, and wilfully obscure. What attracted me was the aura of rebellion that surrounded them: a punk rock rejection of the corporate model of big-budget videogames in favour of the personal, the handmade, the iconoclastic.

The universe seemed to be telling me I was wrong. Maybe indie games were not a force of youthful energy, but a sign that this youthful energy was giving out. It occurred to me that maybe indie games were the bald spot on the head of the videogame industry.

When I was finally able to reorient myself, I began to focus on more mundane matters: namely, how totally unprepared I was for my trip to meet indie-game royalty Craig D. Adams, the mysterious genius known as Superbrothers. I had forgotten to pack T-shirts. I had forgotten to pack deodorant. Possibly because I was a budding academic and not a real journalist, I had forgotten to pack a notebook and a pen. And there was something else. I'd known this all along, but it struck me with real force for the first time then: I knew absolutely nothing about videogames.

I hadn't played one seriously since high school. After my lecture on *Sword & Sworcery* that morning, to a class of Concordia undergraduates studying contemporary Canadian literature, a student had asked me, 'Have you thought about any of this in relation to any *other* videogames?' I don't remember what I said, but the honest answer was no, because I hadn't played any.

After my lecture, I met up with a friend, a musician named Laurel Sprengelmeyer, who records under the name Little Scream. While we were catching up, she asked me what I was doing the next day.

'I'm going to interview a videogame designer guy for a book I'm writing,' I told her.

'I don't really play videogames,' she said.

'Me neither. Well, this one is incredible. It has these beautiful hi-fi/lo-fi graphics and an amazing soundtrack by Jim Guthrie. It's called *Sword & Sworcery.*'

Her face lit up. She slowly and dramatically reached into her back pocket, took out her phone, pressed some buttons, then held it up to me like a charmed sword. On the screen was an 8-bit medieval stick figure set against a techno-pastoral backdrop. Skronky electronic music played.

It was *Sworcery!*

'This is literally the only game I've ever bought,' she said. 'I love it. It's beautiful. The music is incredible. But I'm a little lost. Maybe you can help me.'

That's when I knew that this, too, would be okay. Unlucky in baldness, lucky in books. My book would be for gamers, saying to them what Nico said on the first Velvet Underground record: 'I'll be your mirror, reflect what you are' – show you your metaphorical bald spots. And it would be for Laurel and me and all the people like us who loved art and culture but had only ever bought one videogame.

PART I

UP AND DOWN THE MOUNTAIN

1.

Sword & Sworcery – the 2011 videogame co-released by Superbrothers, musician Jim Guthrie, and independent games studio Capybara – begins in mystery. There's a pleasant whooshing sound, a column of light descends into a pixellated forest, and your avatar emerges from it. All the game tells you to do, in text superimposed on the forest, is 'Look' and 'Listen.' As the game unfolds, you don't learn a whole lot more. You are the Scythian, a warrior sent on a woeful and woefully unspecific errand to the Caucasian mountain of Mingi Taw. Eventually, after solving a series of oblique audiovisual puzzles, you complete the errand, and you die.

Sitting on the bus that morning in October 2013, heading into the woods of Quebec to meet Craig D. Adams, a.k.a. Superbrothers, I pictured myself as the Scythian. I had almost no idea what sort of adventure I was embarking on. Besides a Skype interview conducted in front of my 'Digital Text' class and a few emails to set up the visit, I'd never met Craig. I had signed a contract to write a book on his next game, but I had absolutely no idea what it was going to be like. I wasn't a journalist. I knew next to nothing about videogames.

'Look,' I told myself. 'Listen.'

The night before, Craig had written me an email about what to expect on the bus ride – I was to look out for an 'ok-sized mountain' and a chicken restaurant. I took out my newly purchased notebook and started taking notes. On my right-hand side, I saw a flat rural landscape that reminded me of southwestern Ontario, where I grew up: fields of wheat and corn, trees whose leaves were changing colour. Pretty soon, though, on the left, I started to see some isolated hills, sitting on the flatness like loaves of bread on a table. After a while there were mountains on both sides, all covered in snow, which gave the sense of entering not just a different region but a different season. It was the first snow I'd seen since the previous March.

The symbolic overtones deepened when I saw an exit sign for a ski resort called Bromont. Brother Mountain. *Super*-brother Mountain. Once you get these kinds of resonances into your head, it's hard to stop. The town I was travelling to, Magog, didn't make it any better. I knew enough of the Bible from studying English literature to know that 'Gog and Magog' were bywords for the unfathomable and the apocalyptic: monsters, evil nations, twin-city twins of Sodom and Gomorrah. Before leaving for the bus stop that day, I'd looked the legend up on Wikipedia, where I was informed that Magog is effectively a synonym for Scythia, the homeland of *Sworcery*'s protagonist. *Magogia*, in fact, is the Greek word for Scythia, referring not so much to a literal place as to all the unknown things that lay beyond the northern boundaries of the Greek imagination. That northern boundary corresponded, more or less, to the Caucasus mountains – the setting for *Sworcery* and, in the real world, the chain that runs from the Black Sea to the Caspian Sea and sealed Persia from the unknown lands beyond.

I wasn't just travelling to meet a videogame designer. I was travelling into his videogame.

Eventually, after an hour and a half or so, the bus pulled into a chicken restaurant at the side of the road, and I met Craig in person for the first time.

When you talk to someone on Skype, even though you're seeing their face and hearing their voice, the experience is sufficiently flat and low-res that your imagination takes over, and you begin to see what you want to see. Going into my in-class Skype interview with Craig the previous winter, I'd thought of him as the mysterious hipster genius who made the moody, angular, post-punk videogame I'd assigned to my class. My first digital glimpse of him confirmed this preconception. I'd never met him while we were both living in Toronto, but he looked pretty much like my Toronto friends. He was obviously indoors but was incongruously dressed for winter: the shoulders-up view revealed a toque and a navy wool double-breasted peacoat with gold buttons. His outfit seemed designed to defy the inside/outside distinction in the same way that our Skype chat was defying the dualities of here/there and presence/absence. It was terrifically avant-garde. He was exactly the person I'd hoped he would be.

Now, in person, right away I saw that he was someone quite different.

From my seat in the bus, I looked down on a medium-sized line of bus-greeters outside St. Hubert's. At the back of the line was a tall and somewhat awkward person. He was wearing the same toque from the Skype chat, which in this context was clearly no kind of fashion statement but simply a way of keeping his head warm. He had on huge aviator glasses, presumably as protection from snow-glare while driving. And he wore a ratty red Gore-Tex jacket of the kind owned, for practical reasons, by every person I've ever met from the West Coast (Craig is from West Vancouver) – but worn, for aesthetic reasons, by no East Coast hipster ever. My first journalistic observation of consequence was that Craig, contrary to the strong impression created by *Sworcery* and extrapolated from our Skype chat, was not – or was no longer – a hipster.

I got out of the bus. It was way too cold for my thin East Coast hipster Barbour jacket. I introduced myself. Craig said hello and handed me a gift: a small package of locally made 'Skouik! Skouik!' brand cheese curds, named, onomatopoeically, for the sound they make when you chew them. For all my appreciation of artistic geniuses, another worry that had cropped up during the bus ride was that it might be unpleasant to spend a whole weekend with one. What if Craig turned out to be an asshole? So the gift came as a relief, for it is an immutable fact of logic that a person who brings a stranger a cleverly branded package of local cheese cannot be an asshole.

Not a hipster, then, and not an asshole – but what? My immediate impression of Craig was as a kind of ideal monk. He struck me as humble, calm, respectful, incorruptible, earnest, and steadfastly devoted to a cause. He was gentle but he would fight for what was right. I could easily picture his pale features – his barely perceptible eyebrows the same colour as his skin, his light eyes – framed by the brown hood of a Hieronymite's tunic.

We got in his car, an oldish suv, and we set out on the long drive from Magog to his house. I opened the package of cheese and began skouiking. The landscape was rolling, with snowy hills and freezing lakes. Craig explained that this was a popular summer vacation area, particularly for well-off English speakers from Montreal, such as Mordecai Richler, who had owned a cottage nearby. After we'd chit-chatted about Montreal, music, Little Scream, and Arcade Fire, I made it clear to him that my experience in videogames was very slight. I had played a lot of Nintendo as a kid, but my sister was so much better than me that I'd increasingly spent time outside playing sports. Once, in high school, I'd broken my collarbone snowboarding and spent a few weeks obsessively playing TIE *Fighter*, to the point where all my dreams played out in a videogame landscape, an experience that I found sufficiently disturbing that I stayed well clear of videogames after I recovered.

He seemed relieved. He said he was tired of talking with fanboys and engaging in contests of have-you-played-this-game-okay-but-have-you-played-*this*-one? With *Sworcery,* and especially with his new project, he was interested in my precise demographic: people who had played videogames as kids, sworn them off in favour of other activities and art forms, and might now be tempted to return to them. People like my friend Laurel and, if you've continued reading this far, in all probability people like you.

I was relieved, too, as one is when apparent deficiencies turn into unexpected advantages. We talked about high school. I figured out that he was three years older than me.

Eventually we came to the minuscule town where he lives. Its name doesn't appear on maps. There is a church, a firehall, a general store, and a few roads circling the western margin of a big lake, one shore of which is dominated by a massive jutting cliff face that I will call The Summit. Outside the general store there was a sign advertising deer urine for sale – something to do with hunting.

After a minute or so, we came to the house, a peaked-roof 1980s construction with a log-cabin feel, slightly away from the lake on a dirt road. Craig and his wife had recently settled on a name for it, Ghostwood Lodge, a reference to *Twin Peaks*. Inside, Craig made us coffees in his espresso maker, and, before I was able to get my bearings, I found myself involved in an intense discussion of *Indie Game: The Movie*, the genre-defining 2012 documentary. Craig is one of those people who is much more comfortable talking about huge, abstract ideas than engaging in small talk. I'm a good listener, so we got along.

Indie Game: The Movie didn't name or invent indie games, but it quickly became the standard account of the genre. The argument of IGTM is that independent production transformed videogames from a form of entertainment to a form of artistic expression. In the bad old days, from the 1960s to the recent past, it took huge teams, massive budgets, and unfathomable technical skills to make a videogame. Since they were so expensive to make, studios tended to make conservative artistic choices, sticking to the genres and stories they knew would sell. Since the people with the technical skills to make games were mostly young and male and white – as were the people running the game studios and the people buying the games – diversity of perspective was minimal, and the videogame world became an increasingly insular feedback loop.

Two things conspired to break this mould. First was the emergence of relatively easy-to-use game making tools (also called 'game engines'), which significantly reduced the technical threshold. Second was the development of online marketplaces for games, which eliminated the need for creators to work through the cumbersome and gatekeeper-laden gauntlet of console licencing deals, cartridge manufacture, and brick-and-mortar retail sales. Valve's Steam and Apple's App Store made it possible for normal people to upload their games and reach their audience with little intervening fuss, and forced the hands of Microsoft, Sony, and Nintendo, each of which opened their own channels for digital distribution. By the mid-2000s, independent games had reached a tipping point: it was possible, with a team as small as one person, to make a game that could attract a huge audience. Games like Jonathan Blow's *Braid* (2008), Edmund McMillen and Tommy Refenes's *Super Meat Boy* (2010), and Phil Fish and Renaud Bédard's *Fez* (2012) – the three games that IGTM focuses on – showed that weird, risky, seemingly uncommercial games could make their creators millions.

IGTM's big argument is that independent production has given game designers the ability to take artistically significant risks, just like independent filmmakers, musicians, and writers. Tommy Refenes makes the case when he says, 'We sort of get to do what we want. We don't have publishers, we don't have investors, we don't *answer* to anybody. [...] We get away with a lot of stuff.' This argument, attractive as it is, falls apart a bit when you look at the details of his game, *Super Meat Boy*. The things it gets away with are middle fingers, cartoonish gore, and endless references to the video-games McMillen and Refenes played as kids. Personally, I find it hard to imagine fans of Agnès Varda, Can, or Kathy Acker being drawn to its intensely self-referential world of bloody saws, tricky mechanics, and girlfriends who need to be rescued by boyfriends.

I've found that non-gamers respond much more to another of IGTM's arguments: the surprisingly surprising notion that video-games are made by people. Even those inside the videogame world tend not to think of games as the products of individuals. Instead, their fandom unfolds in relation to studios: they like Looking Glass, or Bethesda, or Naughty Dog. The most revolutionary thing about IGTM is that it puts faces to the process of making a video-game, and it shows that the people who make them experience all the usual emotions connected with artistic creation: the urge for self-expression, the desire to communicate, the agonies of self-doubt and failure, the rapture of success. The revelation of IGTM for most non-gamers is that videogames can be personal – that they can express their creators' 'flaws and vulnerabilities,' as Jonathan Blow puts it. Its most convincing argument for *indie* games is that small teams and small budgets are far more likely to produce these kinds of personal games.

In IGTM, Jonathan Blow provides the theory, and Phil Fish acts it out. Blow, a soft-spoken, slightly lisping San Franciscan in a beige Hawaiian shirt, comes across mostly as what he is, a particularly thoughtful and literate programmer. Fish, a hirsute Montréalais madman in a striped sweater, is immediately recognizable as an artist, without any need for an asterisk or an adjective. He's a cantankerous, sensitive egomaniac whose urgent need to impress and confound is reflected in the constantly changing patterns of his facial hair. Long shots follow him engaging in all the stereotyped poses of the enervated genius: he floats on his back in a pool, gazing into the distance with barely suppressed rage; he broods at a bar, longing, pondering, on the edge of a sob or a guffaw. In one scene, he threatens to kill a former collaborator who hasn't signed the legal documents dissolving their partnership. In another, describing the endless delays that his perfectionism has produced, he promises to kill himself if he doesn't meet his next deadline.

Craig told me there are two things he doesn't like about IGTM. The first is the title. He hates the genre label 'indie game,' which the film helped set in stone. 'Indie' sounds flimsy and ephemeral, unbearably white and saccharine, evoking Adam Brody listening to Death Cab for Cutie on his headphones in his rich parents' SoCal mansion, in skinny jeans and the Chucks he bought at the mall. Craig preferred 'DIY' or 'Do-It-Yourself videogames,' which suggested instead the aggressively countercultural, justice-seeking, empowered self-production of the early punk scene.

The second is that it disrespects Toronto. The pioneers of the local scene – Jessica Mak, Raigan Burns, and Mare Sheppard, who were releasing hit indie games before Blow's *Braid* – aren't mentioned. The only Torontonian who makes it into the movie, Jason DeGroot, is the former partner that Fish says he wants to murder. He isn't named, appearing only in a digitally blocked-out photograph – as a 'pixellated ghost,' in Craig's words. The only Toronto game mentioned in the film is *Sworcery*, a short clip overlaid with a bold textual rendering of the game's revenue at the time of IGTM's release, $1 million. When IGTM came out, the Toronto indie-game scene felt angry and excluded. The bad feelings lingered and were among the reasons Craig decided to leave the city and head for the woods.

Was it the main reason, I asked?

No, he said, not at all. Being from BC, he had always wanted to be back around mountains and lakes, and his wife Jori had always wanted to come back to the community where she'd grown up. But there were blockages. How would you make a living in the woods? How would you stay in touch with the world without high-speed internet? The success of *Sworcery* – and the arrival of fibre-optic lines in rural Quebec – removed the blockages. They decided to get married and move to the woods.

In that magical year of 2011, he said, 'All of my dreams really came true: the wedding, making a pixel-art videogame with Jim Guthrie, being able to rub shoulders with industry legends. Where do you go from there? You say, "Okay, I don't need to chase after that anymore. What I need to do is actually take a little bit of time and dream new dreams."'

(In late September 2021, ten years on from that *annus mirabilis*, I asked him if he could remember the dream as it then looked to his younger self. 'I wanted to live in the woods with Jori,' he said, 'and have a family and work on a project that was sustaining and challenging for a long period of time with a great friend of mine, and have it be low-complexity and low-stress – which it was,' he added, 'for a number of years.')

2.

After we'd finished our coffee and our assessment of the documentary, Craig suggested a hike up the Summit. We put on our coats and got on some bikes, which we rode to the trailhead. We headed for the centre of the town and its three buildings: church, fire hall, and general store. We left our bikes unlocked outside the store, in front of which hung a bilingual and gloriously unspecific sign, 'Magasin GENERAL Store.'

We climbed up a short, paved road, dipped down a path, and entered a leafless deciduous forest poised between fall and winter.

As we started to climb, Craig asked me how the lecture in Montreal had gone. This wasn't quite the same as asking me what the lecture was about, but I couldn't resist giving him a summary. This came not so much from a desire to show off as the need to confess – not from an inflated ego but from a guilty conscience.

This guilty conscience came, basically, from having studied English. Your job as an English undergrad is to make brilliant arguments, whether you think they're true or not. Since the notion of objective or universal truth is the first casualty of English programs, your job isn't to seek the facts, but to make a compelling argument. Obviously, there is something perverse about dedicating all your time to brilliant performances of opinions you don't hold, but since I, like many of us, work on the writings of dead people, there aren't usually any consequences. I could say whatever I wanted about them, with no chance of offending them or misrepresenting their intentions, since these were forever sealed in their graves. It was in this mode that I'd cooked up my grand theory about *Sworcery*.

I was motivated first and foremost by a desire to come up with something interesting to say. One thing I'd noticed in teaching

'The Digital Text' was that 'kids today' were a lot less into high-tech stuff – iPads, e-books, electronic literature, videogames – than I'd expected. I thought my students wanted to be hackers, but what they really wanted to be was Renaissance printers, inking type and pressing it into handmade paper. I'd been searching for some grand, arty way of selling *Sworcery* to them when I happened to see Lars von Trier's *Melancholia* at the TIFF Bell Lightbox. The movie absolutely floored me – the mood, the music, the ever-present rumble of the rogue planet about to smash into Earth – but what gave me an idea was its endless references to opera, in particular to Wagner's *Tristan und Isolde*.

When I got home, I dug out one of my old essays from my undergrad days on Nietzsche, Wagner, and opera. I did a bit more digging and it all fell into place: a big, huge, unlikely argument about the relationship between indie games and Wagnerian opera. More specifically, that Craig himself was the twenty-first-century Wagner – that he had done for videogames what Nietzsche claimed Wagner had done for opera.

Everyone who heard me say it liked it, and it all hung together in my head. But I had no idea if it was true. Only Craig knew that. And he was about to tell me.

My lecture started with the two great clichés about videogames: that they are important because they are interactive, and that they're new because they're 'multimedia.' In an interactive game, you're no longer just the reader: you get to 'be' a character in the story as well, and since your actions directly affect the course of the narrative, you're also a kind of author. In a multimedia game, there is no longer any question of separating arts like writing, painting, filmmaking, photography: they all merge into a single combined digital soup. As Phil Fish says in *Indie Game: The Movie*, videogames are 'the sum total of every expressive medium of all times, made interactive.' Fish finds this tremendously exciting: 'How is that not…? – It's awesome! I want to be a part of it! I want to have a say in what becomes of videogames.'

Sworcery pushes back hard against both these standard ways of looking at videogames. It's not interested in giving you the feeling that you have been magically merged with the character you play (the Scythian) or that you're in charge of the story. The narrative is told in the second-person plural 'we.' When, following a conversation with the character Logfella early in the game, the player is told, 'We definitely [get] the feeling that he [wasn't] super jazzed about this,' the pronoun 'we' plays into that old notion – interactivity's fantasy of union, whereby 'we,' player and character and author, are bound together in a warm, fuzzy tangle. But as things progress, the game goes out of its way to remind us that this fantasy is just that, a fantasy. *Sworcery* is famously reluctant to explain itself to its player or give hints, but when it does, the instructions come in the form of oblique statements – 'We thought that maybe we oughta go investigate the meadow where the sheep used to be' – where it's pretty clear that one part of 'us' (the game's creators) knows a whole lot more about what we should be doing than the other part of 'us.'

This breaking-apart of the cheery 'we' into a series of gloomy 'I's provides the emotional core of the game's heartbreaking ending. At one point, we discuss with another character 'Why we wandered here in this mountain wilderness & how we were guided by the finger of an all-knowing god.' Once again, one part of 'us' knows a lot more than the other. Though she, the character, doesn't seem to realize it, we, the player, are the 'all-knowing god' in question: it's we who've been acting like a god or a tyrant, tip-tapping her around in this world like a ragdoll, with no will of her own. There's a power imbalance in our second-person plural, and we're the beneficiaries. We have all the control, and the Scythian has none. By the start of the last sequence, the plural 'we' disappears completely. The game's narrator tells us, 'It was very brave & generous to offer to martyr the Scythian atop Mingi Taw.' In other words, you, the player, are using your power advantage over her to do the least generous thing imaginable: you are killing her. In the next screen, the game says, 'Press play if you're ready to bear witness to the awful torment of martyrdom,' and invites us to click on a right-pointing triangle. You need to click the play icon to beat the game, but the game wants you to think long and hard before you do. Rather than offering some comfy merging of character and author, it places us in an ethical snake pit: the only way to gratify our selfish desire to win is by ending someone else's life.

That was my first point about *Sworcery*: it is not trying to be your friend. It isn't out to confirm the comfortable old clichés about videogames: it exists to challenge them. And if it has to make you, the player, uncomfortable along the way, so be it. In other words, *Sworcery* is an *avant-garde* videogame. Way back in 1913, Italian poet F. T. Marinetti described his avant-garde movement, Futurism, as 'an inexhaustible machine gun pointing at the army of the dead, of the gouty and the opportunists, whom we' – Marinetti and his crew of Futurists – 'want to strip of their authority and subject to the bold and creative young.' *Sworcery* maybe isn't quite 'an inexhaustible machine gun' – it's a little too self-aware and arch to describe in such military terms. But the avant-garde impulse is definitely there. It's trying to stir shit up.

Of course, every good avant-garde movement needs a manifesto (Marinetti certainly wrote a few), and so the next part of my lecture focused on 'Less Talk, More Rock,' a polemical essay Craig published on the website *Boing Boing* in March 2010, exactly a year before *Sworcery* was released. The essay is a straight-up, over-the-top attack on mainstream 'AAA' videogames – a term for glossy games in established genres with budgets in the tens or hundreds of millions of dollars (fittingly, it comes from the credit industry's bond ratings, where 'AAA' refers to the safest of safe bets). Its problem with these games, as the title suggests, is that they are dominated by 'talk,' which in the manifesto has two meanings. In big studios, too much time is spent debating a game's central idea, discussing whether it will sell, blah blah blah. In the process, anything original about a game is watered down and destroyed. So this is an 'indie' argument: take away the bloated corporate structures of the big studios, and you might get some actual bold ideas in videogames.

The second type of 'talk' takes place in the games themselves. Craig would rather be 'seeing things, hearing things, spotting patterns, flowing through spaces, experiencing moods and locations,' he writes, but too often the experience is 'pierced by disruptive, dissonant elements: overlong and condescending tutorials, over-explained idiotic stories and a million other stupidities.' With an almost Marinettian vehemence, he writes,

> To me these kinds of things are repulsive, evidence of a deficient imagination or a lack of videogame literacy on the part of the creator, or simply evidence of a committee. These things break the spell, they're an invitation to quit, and they exist in 99% of the videogames I've played.

I found all the 'talk' talk interesting enough, but it was a different argument in the manifesto that really caught my attention. This one has to do with that other endlessly discussed aspect of the videogame medium, multimedia. Craig's claim here is that critics have been too quick to celebrate videogames' seamless integration of image, video, text, and sound – of 'every expressive medium of all time.' Craig finds the combination of media in most videogames clunky and inept. 'An entire generation,' he writes, 'seems to have become used to experiences clogged with menus and text, spammed with awkward cutscenes, choked by voice acting, mangled by incongruent narrative, segmented by load times, stalled by informational messages.' As videogame machines have become more and more powerful, with better sound, smoother movement, and more detailed graphics, creators have lagged in their ability to combine these meaningfully. The result, Craig writes, in one of the most memorable parts of the essay, is a generation of creators and players addicted to 'bloated cross-media confections.'

What Craig was saying about videogames today was almost exactly what Richard Wagner and Friedrich Nietzsche said in the nineteenth century about the exciting new multimedia form of their own day: the opera. It is hard (for me, and perhaps for you, too) to see why someone would get excited about opera, even as recently as 150 years ago. But, back then, people were excited about it, and it was mostly because its multimedia-ness was seen as innovative. The name 'opera' comes from a pluralization of *opus*, a work of art. The word entered the English language in the seventeenth century, when it was defined as 'a composition in which poetry, dance, and music are combined' (painting and sculpture also sneak in, through set design). By the time of Wagner and Nietzsche, the opera was the AAA videogame of the time: a hugely popular and absolutely bloated cross-media confection that threw every art form together into a sweet and delectable smorgasbord of entertainment.

Like Craig in 2010, Wagner and Nietzsche back then were not amused. In his 1849 pamphlet *Art and Revolution*, Wagner looked around at the operas of his day and concluded that they were no more than an 'inane patchwork,' a 'chaos of sensuous impressions jostling one another without rhyme or reason.' Creators had a powerful new medium to work with, and audiences were gobbling it up, but they were making a mess of it – they didn't understand their form well enough to do anything important with it. This is the most interesting thing about Wagner's and Nietzsche's writing about opera: they believed, to an absolutely maniacal degree, that *important things could be done with opera*. Wagner, for example, thought that a perfected version of the opera could pave the way for a perfect society. The problem with opera as it stood was that all the individual arts weren't meshing. But if each of them could be made to work together to deliver a common message, the opera would stand as a model for a socialist utopia where people sacrifice their selfish desires to the common good. As Wagner said in *Art and Revolution* (because, yes, he thought his operas would bring one about), the 'perfect Art-work' would mirror the 'united utterance of a free and lovely public.'

The mad philosopher Friedrich Nietzsche got incredibly excited about Wagner's ideas. His first book, *The Birth of Tragedy*, is a long, thrilling, unhinged explanation of why Wagnerian opera was about to usher in a new phase of world history. For Nietzsche, there are two types of artistic experience: the Dionysian and the Apollinian. The first – named for the Greek god of wine, theatre, and ecstasy – is art as drunkenness, rapture, the destruction of the ego and dissolution of the will. Think of a rave, where loud, rhythmic music has just as powerful an effect as actual alcohol (or Dionysus's more modern invention, MDMA) in making you feel that your individuality is merging into some form of group consciousness. Under the sway of the Dionysian, Nietzsche says, the spectator 'feels himself not only reconciled, and fused with his neighbour, but as one with him.' The second type of experience, the Apollinian, is named for the Greek god of poetry and light. Rather than shattering the ego, the Apollinian strengthens our sense of ourselves as individuals through its qualities of clarity, realism, and beauty. Think of the experience of looking at a sculpture in a museum – perhaps Bernini's *Apollo and Daphne* in the Galleria Borghese in Rome. You walk around it, taking it in from all angles, admiring the accuracy of the representation, where nothing is hidden or mysterious and everything is lovely, comprehensible, perfectly rendered. Rather than a feeling of drunken rapture, the experience is calm, sober, dignified. You admire from a distance, without being drawn in. Your ability to contemplate at a remove reinforces your sense that you are one thing and the sculpture is another, absolutely separate.

What excited Nietzsche so much about Wagner was that he had managed to *balance* the Dionysian and the Apollinian. Nietzsche thought all other operas sacrificed the Dionysian to the Apollinian: there was no thunder, it was all happy, sappy, neat, and tidy. With Wagner, there was thunder. Nietzsche argued that Wagner used music in his operas to create the Dionysian rapture – and used poetry to inspire the Apollinian experience of beauty and composure. In Wagnerian opera, as in no artistic form since the Greek tragedy, it was not an either/or: Wagner gave you both the great artistic impulses at the same time, neither dominating over the other.

My theory was that *Sworcery* was trying to do the same thing. The standard line on videogames was that they broke down oppositions: between player, creator, and character; between music, graphics, text. It seemed to me that *Sworcery* was very deliberately trying *not* to break these oppositions down but to set them against one another – to keep each one distinct and to make them clash. And I had a theory that Nietzsche's ideas had actually inspired *Sworcery*'s approach.

My clue was a line on the 'About' page of the *Sworcery* website. Discussing the decision to make the Scythian a woman, Craig explains that this 'may have something to do with Leonard Schlain's *The Goddess & The Alphabet: The Conflict Between Text and Image.*' Though it took me some time to track down a copy of Leonard Shlain's *The Alphabet Versus the Goddess: The Conflict Between Word and Image* (yes, Craig had managed to muddle the author's name, the title, and the subtitle), when I found it, I was overcome with joy. Not because it is a good book – it is quite bad – but because it is essentially a rewriting of Nietzsche's *Birth of Tragedy*.

Shlain, a neurosurgeon by trade, maps the Apollinian and the Dionysian onto the left and right brain: the left hemisphere is the site of logical, Apollinian processes of linear timekeeping, whereas the right hemisphere is given over to Dionysian tasks like global awareness, pattern recognition, and non-verbal communication. Shlain argues that the invention of writing privileged the Apollinian left brain, which was needed to decode linear sequences of letters, whereas the arrival of television and videogames, by appealing to right-brain Dionysian impulses, would rebalance the human sensorium. (Shlain's real theory is that this mental recalibration will promote feminism, but this argument makes so little sense, and is based on such flimsy pseudo-science, that I won't bother to repeat it here. Maybe that's why Craig muddled everything so spectacularly, as a kind of oblique asterisk, an ortho-graphical *achtung*.)

Shlain's quasi-Nietzschean ideas are behind some of the most remarkable aspects of *Sworcery*. The game's signature mechanic – the way that it makes you wait for real-life moon phases to unlock areas for exploration – is clearly Shlain-derived. It exists to slow us down, to encourage us to set aside our linear, left-brain, Apollinian haste to speed through the plot – to take the time to 'see things, hear things, spot patterns, flow through spaces, experience moods and locations.' The boss battles at the end of every sequence work similarly: yes, they're inescapably linear, they're obstacles to overcome on the way to beating the game, but at the same time the best way to beat them is to chill out, turn down your competitive urge to advance, and listen to the music, whose rhythms contain the vital clues for how to progress. Same with the many audiovisual puzzles you need to solve to release sylvan sprites: if you're in a 'blasting-through' headspace, you'll never chill out enough to think of playing a waterfall like a guitar, or to look for microscopic discrepancies between a grove of trees and its reflection in a pool. To accomplish the Apollinian task of beating *Sworcery*, you need to open the door to the Dionysian.

Why are all these people – Wagner, Nieztsche, Shlain, Craig – so obsessed with art that can balance opposing impulses in the mind of its audience? Wagner thought this kind of art would usher in a new society. So did Nietzsche: the upshot of *The Birth of Tragedy* is nothing less than the triumph of the German nation. About Wagnerian operas like *Tristan und Isolde* he wrote, 'What hopes must revive in us when the most certain auspices guarantee […] *the gradual awakening of the Dionysian spirit* in our modern world!' adding, 'Let no one try to blight our faith in a yet-impending rebirth of Hellenic antiquity; for this alone gives us hope for a renovation and purification of the German spirit through the fire magic of music.' (One of my personal rules: take any statement containing the expression 'fire magic' with an extra grain of salt.)

The creators of *Sworcery* most certainly didn't think that it would carry out anything like 'the renovation and purification of the Canadian spirit' – because, let's not be silly. But they seemed to earnestly believe it had the power to change the world. Videogame theorist Ian Bogost argues that what is most exciting about videogames, compared with all other art forms, is that instead of *telling you things* or *showing you things*, they make you *act things out*. (Bogost's overly fancy name for this relatively simple facet of videogame magic is 'procedural rhetoric.') This idea helped me see what is so powerful in *Sworcery*. Nietzsche and Shlain try really hard to *convince us* of the value and necessity of balancing our minds, of giving the Apollinian and Dionysian, left and right brain, equal weight.

But *Sworcery* is a machine for achieving that balance. To progress through the game, you need to stop trying to progress through the game. The ideal player holds Apollo in one hand and Dionysus in the other. No collapsed binaries, just messy contradictions and equally valid opposites.

This is the ideal player of *Sworcery*, and it's the sort of player that *Sworcery* manufactures.

It doesn't matter to me whether *Sworcery* actually changed the world. Millions of people downloaded *Sworcery* on June 9, 2013, when it was available for free as part of the fifth-anniversary celebrations for the Apple App Store. Did these millions of people subsequently experience the rebalancing of their minds? Should we expect a new world order?

What matters is that the creators of *Sworcery* believed they could change the world.

They had a well-thought-out plan for using art as a vehicle for mass psychological change, they decided a videogame was the best vehicle for it, and they put their plan in motion. This places *Sworcery* in an artistic lineage that I admire and that I understand: a lineage that starts with people like Nietzsche, passes through Virginia Woolf, Wallace Thurman, Walter Benjamin,

Bertolt Brecht, W. H. Auden, Charles Mingus, Marshall McLuhan, Poly Styrene, Kathy Acker, Werner Herzog, Kathleen Hanna, David Lynch.

It places *Sworcery* in the tradition of the avant-garde: people who used art to change the world, and probably succeeded. This tradition includes books of philosophy and criticism, novels, poems, paintings, films, seven-inches, LPS, zines – but as far I could figure, as far as I personally knew, this might just have been the first videogame in the tradition, the first of its kind to participate in the noble brainwashing enterprise that is avant-garde art. To quote Phil Fish again: 'How is that not…? – It's awesome!'

Or so my lecture went.

The path up the Summit is narrow and, that day, was covered in snow. I was walking behind Craig, stepping in his two-inch-deep footprints to save energy and to avoid slipping, delivering my lecture to the back of his red coat. It must have been a shorter version than what's set out above, because that climb couldn't have taken more than twenty minutes. But I do remember hitting all the main points: the unstable 'we,' Wagner and Nietzsche, Apollo and Dionysus, Shlain, manifestos, the avant-garde.

Craig nodded or commented a few times, but mostly he let me talk, without looking back, and the longer I talked to his back, the more far-fetched my theory seemed – the more it felt like a projection of my own desires than an honest interpretation of the game. But as we neared the top, he looked back and smiled, said that these ideas were indeed in his head as he was making the game, told me an anecdote about playing Wagner in his high school orchestra, told me about the professor at Sheridan College who'd introduced him to Shlain, and laughed about the reaction to 'Less Talk, More Rock.' A few years later, I published the full version of my theory in a chapter of my book *Literature in the Digital Age*, and by this time we knew one another well enough for him to send me a line-by-line reaction:

oooh *sworcery* here we go
ooooh 'polemical essay'
oh boy, i sure said some stuff back in the day
i haven't read nietzsche but i get what he means about wagner
sworcery sounds so smart and fancy
but yes all these thoughts were certainly on my mind!
apollo/dionysus is right there in the title
aside, the 'procedural rhetoric' 'mechanic + theme' aspects that i think i like the most are:
-how the scythian is worn down as a reward for her noble efforts, the player notices and has to kind of quietly accept and inhabit that
-the strange questioning of the player's role as relentless unknowable taskmaster that emerges in session IV
but anyways
i love all of this!
you write real nice

(A note to reviewers of this book: 'I love all of this; you write real nice' is a great starting point.)

I didn't have much time to bask in my surprise, or relief, or the possibility that I'd found an intellectual soulmate, because we had come to the top of The Summit. On our right was a clearing. In a reversal of perspective, I found myself looking down from the top of the massive rock face I'd earlier seen from across the lake.

The mountain itself looked so much like Mingi Taw from *Sworcery* that I expected a mouth to open in the cliff face at any moment, revealing a secret path. Unlike in the videogame, though, I could look out from the mountain as well as in. Below us was a long, rolling landscape, neat alternating squares of white and green bordered by property lines and roadways, extending into the distance. Down to our right were the three buildings of the town, so small now that they looked like models in a fancy department store's electric train display. Straight across, not so far from the lake's western shore, was Craig's house.

He stepped right up to the edge, but it was too high and steep for me. He stood at the edge by himself for a while, and when he came back, he told me a story he'd just remembered.

June 2000 was a turning point in his life. After graduating high school in 1997, he'd done a year of Earth and Ocean Sciences at the University of Victoria. But instead of returning for his second year, he stayed at home, in his parents' house in West Vancouver, played videogames, and, in the winter, moved to Panorama Mountain near the Rockies, where he worked as a cook and spent his free time snowboarding. He also got sucked into the world of the Nintendo 64 classic *Legend of Zelda: Ocarina of Time*. He spent so much time in this world that he began to ask himself what would happen if he played real life like it was a videogame – if he inhabited a world as symbolically dense and meaning-filled as *Zelda*, where every door entered and every coin collected was a step toward the completion of an adventure, and every conversation contained some veiled instruction that could propel you toward your fate if you only had the wits to uncover it. This ultimately led him, in a roundabout way, to making videogames. But he wasn't quite there yet.

Back in Vancouver, he gave university another shot, this time studying Oceanography and Calculus at the University of British Columbia, but he didn't make it through the year. 'This is how you become part of the established order,' he said about university. 'If you have real grievances with the established order, then it's hard to fit in.' Also, university was hard. In high school, he'd floated by with good grades for minimal effort. He thought, 'Oh man, I'm going to need to apply myself – and I don't get along with this all that much, and culturally I just don't want to go down this road and end up a self-satisfied middle-class part-of-the-problem kind of person.' He spent the rest of the year travelling, in Hong Kong, New Zealand, and Australia, where he crossed the continent with a legendary punk roadie whom legendary 'I'll

Be Your Mirror' chanteuse Nico apparently considered her one true love – though that's another story.

From the start, even before enrolling in Earth Sciences and Oceanography, Craig's plan was to eventually go to art school. Since high school, he told me, laughing a bit at his younger self, he'd been working on a multi-part scheme that involved 'learning plant science, and then becoming involved with computers and communications to create an Al Gore's *An Inconvenient Truth*–style multimedia presentation.' Craig was an environmentalist, as I was learning for the first time, and had also seen himself from a young age as an artistic propagandist – one naturally drawn to the 'noble brainwashing enterprise' of the avant-garde. Now, in June 2000, he was contemplating an alteration to the plan: skipping the university science degree and going straight to art school. He picked up a book of Ralph Steadman's drawings, said to himself, 'Okay, this is what I'll do, I'll be an illustrator,' and signed up for the Illustration program at Sheridan College in Oakville, near Toronto.

Yet Craig still felt the need for some kind of firm marker that would commit him to this new path absolutely. His brother and sister, three and six years older than him, had gone to university, and that had worked out for them. Going to art school felt like more of a risk. He'd always had a feeling that things wouldn't work out for him, as they hadn't exactly worked out for his father, who had been on the fringes of the computer business his whole life without establishing himself firmly in that world or making the millions that his contemporaries did. (His father had biographies of Bill Gates and Steve Jobs on his bookshelf but had consistently decided not to invest in Microsoft or Apple.) Craig wanted a way of tying himself to this path so that he couldn't just back out when self-doubt flared up. So the night before registration, he headed to Lighthouse Park in West Vancouver with the plan to jump off a cliff.

Lighthouse Park is one of those Vancouver fantasy places, nearly 200 acres of old-growth rainforest on a rocky spit in the

Strait of Georgia. Craig went there a lot in high school, including at night – you could go to a late movie, then head to the park to look at the stars. On the western edge is Juniper Point, with a big rock cliff used for climbing and jumping. He figured the drop was somewhere around fifty to seventy feet.

It was night, the moon was reflecting off the waves, he was alone. It was not incredibly risky: he'd seen a few people jump over the years. But he'd never tried it himself. The only dangerous things were that he was out alone at night and he hadn't told anyone where he was. It was very likely that he would survive. He told himself that if he could jump off the cliff and make it back to shore, then he would probably be okay on this path. He jumped, it was a really long drop, he hit the water, he got out and climbed back up the rock, put on his clothes, and went back to his car.

The jump gave him strength at Sheridan. It had committed him. The next summer, he was on a canoeing and climbing trip in Killarney Park in northern Ontario and his friends asked him to set up a top rope on a precarious ledge with an overhang. At a certain point, he said, 'No, I'm not doing this. I've put time in on something. I'm building something here. This is a needless risk and I'm not going to take it.'

Craig was on his path.

By the time he finished his story, we'd been up on the Summit for a while and I was freezing. It was time to walk down from Mingi Taw and into real life.

As we started back down, I asked Craig to tell me more about his strategy for using art to change the world. What was the plan, exactly? How had it evolved while he was in art school?

His plan all along was to 'move the needle' on the environment – make a real contribution to how we think about ecology, he told me. His time at UVic and UBC convinced him that a university degree wasn't going to do the trick. When he was back from Australia, he went hiking with a friend in an old-growth forest near Squamish, halfway between Vancouver and Whistler. They heard that a confrontation was brewing between some twenty-year-old activists and a logging company, and they hiked in to witness it. After a while, they tracked down the activists, who told Craig that they'd made a videotape of the company logging the forest illegally. The activists asked Craig to take the tape to a television station in Vancouver. They seemed convinced that this one piece of evidence, this videotape of theirs, if shown on the news, would somehow singlehandedly turn the ecological tide. Faced with such conviction, Craig and his friend could hardly refuse. They took the tape to the news station. Craig couldn't even remember if it made it on the news or not – if it did, it was under a headline along the lines of 'Little kids screw around in forest.' Nothing came of it. The needle wasn't moved.

A thought occurred to him: What if Steven Spielberg had been filming in the forest, not some fringe activist kids? It was a naïve and possibly silly thought, he admitted, but it got him thinking more seriously about whether culture was the way to move that needle – whether you could change the world by changing the way people think, and change the way people think through art. The activists were way over here, Craig told me, and the logging companies were way over there. You needed someone in the middle, someone with cultural and financial capital, someone who people actually wanted to listen to, to bridge that gap. Learn how to make art, and eventually how to make videogames. Work in popular forms, show you can hold an audience, build up a reputation and then, after you've proven yourself, deliver your explicitly environmentalist message. You're twenty-five when you start, maybe you're forty when you shift to the outright activism. That was the plan going into art school and it was still the plan in 2003 when, just before graduating, Craig founded Superbrothers.

The name is meant as a joke, Super Mario Brothers minus Mario, infused in irony and, like much of Craig's work of that time, not to be taken too seriously. But Superbrothers was the vehicle for carrying out his grand mission. The idea was to develop a distinct and recognizable style, spread it as widely as possible through the culture by any means necessary, and then, eventually, do something with it. For Craig, the style was his personal take on pixel art: deliberately jagged, low-res, blocky images to which he added high-res textures, shading effects, and reflections. Laughing at his crazy younger self, he told me that he even came up with a name for his style: 'Rustic 21st Century Minimalism.' Eventually I tracked down Craig's full description of this style on an old, abandoned Facebook page:

STATEMENT: RUSTIC 21ST CENTURY MINIMALISM

Using individual blocks of color to form a precise visual statement is a technique that dates back through the ages at least as far as 4th BCE century Macedonia, arguably reaching its apex with the Christian mosaics of the byzantine empire eight centuries later. It is largely due to the impact of the pixel – that most basic unit of an electronic display – that these grid-based pictures are enjoying a degree of ubiquity in the here and now.

For many among us, this peculiarly abstracted visual language harkens back only as far as the antiquated computer technology & electronic amusements of yesteryear. Necessarily tessellated to accommodate the limited capacities of the machines of that age, the scenarios that were presented in these diversionary programs were nonetheless enchanting, their stories & structures often derived from a rich international tapestry of folktale, myth, imagination & human experience.

As editorial illustration, this imagery is inherently appropriate for subjects related to technology, communication & entertainment. Due to its current visibility in pop culture it has also proven to be an appropriate choice for advertising and fashion applications. As a deliberate mode of artistic representation, in film or in interactive spaces, the painterly SUPERBROTHERS approach to pixel artwork seems to contain a unique expressive power.

Mostly, this is a sendup of an 'Artist's Statement,' which Very Serious Artists need to write to get government grants. The language is extravagant ('necessarily tessellated,' 'diversionary programs') but also contains hints of a very earnest love of the medium he was shifting into – a real affection for the brutally simple yet massively engaging mythic stories he lived out as a kid on his Commodore 64. It is also, of course, an advertisement. It says, 'I, Craig/Superbrothers, a weird and smart and funny illustrator, am available to do my cool pixel art for your magazine or ad campaign or your T-shirt design.'

As we continued back down the narrow path toward the Summit trailhead, he told me about some of the ideas he was working on around the time of 'Rustic 21st Century Minimalism.' This was the phase of the plan where content didn't matter as much as style. He didn't need to be producing his ecological opus, his 'Al Gore's *An Inconvenient Truth*–style multimedia presentation.' So he was coming up with outlandish ideas for videogames that people might actually play and enjoy. (At this point, these were only ideas – Craig didn't know how to program or use game engines to turn his drawings and animations into actual games.) He sketched out an adventure game that would take place along the fifty-three stations of the Tōkaidō, the coastal road that linked Kyoto and the capital in Edo-period Japan; the main action in the game would be haiku battles. Another was a political thriller set on the island of Samos in the year 800 BCE, in the cult of Pythagoras, where the knowledge of irrational numbers was being suppressed. There was a game where you're in the Garden of Eden, with no knowledge whatsoever of what is happening, and the whole action of the game consists of slowly intuiting the rules and goals of this strange place.

Meanwhile, magazine work was paying some bills and advancing the mission. In 2004, only a few months after he founded

Superbrothers, Craig got a gig with *The Walrus*, Canada's answer to *The Atlantic*, a big break. He used one of the images from the Garden of Eden game, a pixellated representation of Adam and Eve, as close to an anatomically correct depiction of two naked people as is possible in the 'tessellated' world of pixels. More work followed in such varied publications as the *New York Times*, *Wired*, ESPN: *The Magazine*, the *Globe and Mail's Report on Business* magazine, and *Runner's World*. The Superbrothers style was in the ether. Craig felt like his plan was working. He was 'infiltrating legitimate publications with pixel art,' as he put it to me. But, alas, impressive as it all sounds, impressive as his resume was becoming, the world of editorial illustration turned out to be not at all lucrative. Pixels didn't pay. He had to take a day job.

But that story would need to wait for after dinner, as we had come to the end of the trail.

3.

Picture a real-life version of Logfella's cabin from *Sworcery*. That's exactly what the inside of Craig's house looked like. I hate to keep leaning on these parallels, but when you have just been escorted up and down Mingi Taw and are now sitting in a living room filled with stags' heads, sipping a homemade Americano, it is your journalistic duty to report them.

One of the stags, massive and carved from wood, was a wedding gift from Jim Guthrie, who did the music for *Sworcery*, and who had found it on Craigslist. Another stag was a real stuffed deer, mounted on a burly plaque, the first kill of a relative of Craig's wife, Jori. Below the wooden stag stood a gorgeous mid-century cabinet into which a record player and stereo had been cunningly integrated. This was the work of Jori, who met Craig in art school, and who is also an artist. She was responsible for the room's many other design flourishes, which included an old printer's type case mounted on the wall and filled with figurines.

After dinner, Craig went upstairs to his office and came down with a USB stick. It was filled with seven gigabytes' worth of background material that he had prepared for me in advance of my visit. The first contained pixels: Adam and Eve, salarymen, stacks of amplifiers. Craig told me about how he'd first met Jim Guthrie. In 2005, while he was still pursuing his illustrator-for-hire path full-bore, he read an article in the Toronto weekly NOW *Magazine* in which writer and local videogame community hero Jim Munroe revealed that local indie-music community hero Jim Guthrie was, as Craig put it, 'a bit of a geek.' Apparently Guthrie spent his time in the tour bus making music on his first-generation Sony PlayStation, using MTV Music Generator and his gamepad. Craig decided to send Jim some of his illustrations and, totally unexpectedly, Jim responded by sending Craig the PlayStation songs. The sense was, 'If you can do something with this, do it.'

A few months later, he did. *Children of the Clone*, completed in 2005, was the first Superbrothers film. It is a parable of corporate self-replication, in which a glad-handing pixellated salaryman recruits an army of briefcase-wielding ignoramuses. Partway through, the ignoramuses revolt, an orgy of righteous violence erupts, corporate blood is spilled, and the salarymen set down their briefcases to dance a stylish and blocky ballet. But, alas, the cycle begins again: the men straighten their ties, and the glad-handing replication resumes. Soundtracking the film is a brilliant fantasia from Guthrie's PlayStation disc built around a sampled one-note guitar riff.

The ironic and over-the-top tone of the early Superbrothers era comes across in a description of *Children of the Clone* that Craig gave around the time of its release:

> I would like the audience to imagine the entire staff of SUPERBROTHERS as a professional team of fifties-era engineers, architects & laborers, t-squares in hand, diligently attacking the complex problems of tessellated representation by manufacturing, assembling and photographing pixel images in a studio or factory setting, at the outskirts of Chicago or, alternately, Minsk. Furthermore, I would like the audience to imagine the first film, THE CHILDREN OF THE CLONE as a surviving relic of this imagined past, a forgotten reel retrieved from the archives of some anonymous government library and retrieved only recently.

In the caption that appears alongside the film on Vimeo, he added,

> Production notes: Very little is known about the creation process of this film, although recently discovered documents retrieved from the Belarusian State University of Informatics

and Radioelectronics suggest that the original reel for the film dated back to the early years of the Stalin era.

The second folder Craig showed me stood in strange contrast with the first. It was full of images from commercial videogames.

At the time he made *Children of the Clone*, Craig was struggling to make ends meet. He took a job working the phones doing tech support for Sony TVs. Seeing that this wasn't heading anywhere, he decided to join the videogame industry. He took another course, 3D Game Design, at Seneca College, finished it, and was immediately hired by Koei Canada, a small Toronto-based studio owned by a large Japanese videogame company. He worked at Koei from late 2006 until mid-2009. His first project there was *Fatal Inertia*, a loosely plotted game that takes place in a dystopian future where the earth is controlled by large corporations that manipulate the masses through extreme sports, the most popular of which is a dangerous hover-car racing game called, you guessed it, Fatal Inertia. Craig's tasks were broad: he worked on lighting, sky textures, camera movement, and sound.

It sounded like the sort of mainstream gig that drives a creative person to indie games. 'It was a mess,' Craig said, 'but I got to try *everything.*' He learned a lot – worked on everything from level design to trailers – and liked his colleagues. Toward the end of his time at Koei, Craig was given heaps of time to develop a video-game adaptation of the foundational text of Western literature, Homer's *Iliad*. The folder Craig showed me contained endless sketches of high-hearted warriors, shining temples, swift warships, and wine-red seas. (In the end, it went nowhere.)

It was at Koei that he started looking for a different model. You need a massive structure, a huge number of employees and huge amounts of money to make a graphics-intensive game like *Fatal Interia*, and in the complicated bureaucracy of a commercial studio, it was hard to get anything done. He also wondered if it was worth doing in the first place. What was the point of a game like *Fatal Inertia*? If it was just to hook people's attention, if it wasn't giving anything back to the player, then it felt unethical to be involved with. 'When you work in the industry,' he said, 'you do have your doubts about what you're doing.'

The solution to this ethical tangle was contained in the third folder, home to the *Sworcery* material.

Toronto didn't have much of a mainstream videogame industry presence in the first decade of the twenty-first century – it was just Koei Canada, really, and they were small and marginal; Ubisoft had not yet arrived. But it had an exploding indie-game scene. Craig was reaching out and making friends – people like Jessica Mak, who made *Everyday Shooter* and would later make *Sound Shapes*, and people like Mare Sheppard and Raigan Burns of Metanet, producers of *N*. In 2008, Craig attended his first TOJam, a yearly three-day pressure cooker of collaboration designed to produce simple games in extreme conditions. After making a zombie game, *The Scourge*, the first year, he returned again in 2009 to make *Alpinist*, a deer-filled pixellated mountain climbing simulator. He also started going to the events put on by the Hand Eye Society, an organization devoted to showcasing and advancing local video-game production. It was also a place to get drunk and make friends.

Throughout this time, Craig was looking around for the right partners. Superbrothers had stalled during his time at Koei, and now he was looking to relaunch it as a DIY videogame brand. The indie infrastructure was in place in Toronto, but he wasn't sure who exactly to work with. In 2009, he attended the Game Developers Conference in San Francisco, the biggest conference in videogames. One night, he bumped into Kris Piotrowski and Nathan Vella, founders of Capybara Games, a.k.a Capy, the Toronto indie-game studio, which at the time had twenty employees. It was the first time they'd met, and they were extremely drunk, but five minutes into their conversation, Nathan said, 'We will make a game together!' Back in Toronto, sober, he still wanted to.

Craig started pitching his idea. He wanted to call it *Poopsock*. Nathan explained that they would need to apply for a grant from the Ontario Media Development Corporation and that 'Poopsock' probably wasn't going to cut it. A few months after meeting at GDC, Craig, Capy, and Jim had submitted their OMDC grant application for a game called *Sword & Sworcery*. The full application package – budget spreadsheets, marketing plans, chains of title, resumes – was in the folder. The game that was eventually released in 2011 is visible in all these documents – but there's also a lot of clutter. In the original plan, there was going to be a whole lot of Facebook integration: there was a 'Monastery' where you could get together a 'Posse' of your *Sworcery*-playing friends, a 'Magic Mirror' to take photos of your in-game appearance, and 'J. R. R. Tokens,' currency you'd accumulate in the game's arcane spaces and use to impress your friends. A lot of space is devoted in the documents to extolling the virtues of a brave new handheld game playing platform, the iPhone. The trend of 'rhythm-based' gameplay features prominently, with many references to Capy's work on the official *American Idol* app. Aside from the reference to Jim Guthrie's adaptive soundtrack as 'Richard Wagner by way of *Castlevania*,' there is little to indicate the game's avant-garde heritage or ambitions. But the grant, which was successful, gave them the financial resources to be weirder than the plan suggested they would be.

Work proceeded. On a thirty-day deadline, they submitted an entry for the 2010 Independent Games Festival, the largest gathering of indie-game developers, part of the broader GDC conference. They won the award for Achievement in Art in a mobile game. Based on a short playable demo and a trailer, this tiny little Canadian game, up against multimillion-dollar blockbusters from all the biggest studios, was widely praised as the most interesting at the conference – not just IGF but the whole of GDC. Craig had agreed to give a short talk at GDC just so that he would get a free badge. But then the talk turned into the 'Less Talk, More Rock' manifesto on *Boing Boing*, and that blew up online.

Now the pressure was incredible. Craig doesn't like to think or talk too much about the rest of 2010, when he was broke and stressed out beyond description. In September 2010, about six months before *Sworcery* launched, he travelled to Austin, Texas, to give a talk at Fantastic Arcade, the newly launched videogame session of the genre-film Fantastic Festival. Though it's hard to tell in the video posted to Vimeo (filmed on Craig's iPhone by Wiley Wiggins, the actor who played the eyebrow-pinching protagonist in Richard Linklater's classic high school stoner film *Dazed and Confused*), Craig told me he hadn't slept in four days before flying to Austin. That pace was typical of the period. He doesn't know how he stayed sane in the last months, or even survived. 'Making a game, man,' he told me. 'Making a game is not easy.'

At GDC 2010, they'd promised *Sworcery* would be released within a few months, when in fact, at that time, all they had was a rough demo build and a seven-minute trailer. Following the substantial post-GDC hype, the pressure to release on time was immense, but it wasn't going to happen. The upside of this was that speculation abounded online about what the finished game might look like. Craig and co. made the most of this, listening closely and turning the best of this speculation into actual features of the game.

By the time of GDC 2011, the game was finally just about ready. Craig had prepared a teaser video, 'Audience Calibration Procedure,' for the event. The voiceover by Toronto-based artist/filmmaker/poet Clive Holden explained the delay: the team had been busy preparing the playing public's subconscious minds for the mental dynamite of *Sworcery*. (The video humbly declared, for instance, that the *real* reason you'd bought an iPhone or iPad was so that you'd be ready to play *Sworcery* when it dropped.) Watching the video was the final step: you were now properly calibrated and ready to participate. Introducing the game's key themes of synchronizing natural and virtual worlds and achieving psychic equilibrium, the video obliquely announced its release date: 'We will meet again at the appointed time, when both day and night are in balance.' For those too dense to get the clue, a quick final frame contained the text, 'WHEN???????????? AROUND THE VERNAL EQUINOX.' Craig came back from GDC 2011 feeling so energized and confident that he immediately proposed to Jori.

On March 24th, 2011, three days after the equinox, with day ever so slightly longer than night, *Sworcery* launched. The game was set to be released at 11 p.m. that Thursday night, but since 11 p.m. in Auckland is 6 a.m. in Toronto, the launch was an all-day event. Craig was working in the Capy office at Spadina and Queen, doing PR work and answering emails. A prominent feature of *Sworcery* is its in-game use of Twitter. Every time a bit of text pops up, you are given the option to tweet it out, with the hashtag #sworcery automatically appended. Since these bits of texts are extremely tweetable, people immediately started tweeting them, albeit in a small way – Craig had to go looking for them. At 6 p.m., the game launched in Europe, and people around the office were saying, 'Hey, cool, people are playing it.' Craig was busy writing emails. It was 8 p.m., then 9 p.m., then on the way out the door he got into a long conversation with Sean Lohrisch, co-founder of Capy. Suddenly it was 10:40 p.m. and the game was about to launch in the Eastern Standard time zone.

When the clock struck eleven, Craig was on the notoriously slow Queen Street streetcar, watching his phone. The reaction was immediate. He didn't need to follow the #sworcery hashtag anymore; everyone he followed seemed to be talking about it. Soon his feed went nuts. He got so engrossed that he missed his stop at Pape, not by one stop, but by ten. He found himself all the way in the Beaches. He didn't want to wait for the streetcar going the other direction – that would take at least half an hour. Walking home would take about the same. He wasn't in the mood for a jog. He was embarrassed about missing his stop but also excited to see that, as he put it, 'It's working.' His first act as the co-creator of a hit videogame was to hail a cab.

Back at home, Jori had been watching the action on Twitter and she was excited, too. They decided they should go somewhere to celebrate. They rounded up some friends who lived nearby and headed around the corner to a bar. For the next several hours, until the bar closed, and then back at their friends' place, they all sat around looking at their phones, shaking their heads in amazement, looking up every now and then to say, 'Can you believe this person is saying this about *Sworcery?*'

There were two main feelings that night.

First, the strange sensation of the private becoming public. 'These are my little paintings that I've been working on my little computer. And now, people all over the place have my paintings, and they're moving around on top of my paintings. The thought of all the people moving their hands and fingers, looking at this artwork that has just been completely private, that was a really weird feeling to reconcile.'

Second, a kind of anticlimax resulting from the immateriality of it all. 'You work on a thing on a computer, you launch the thing and information goes out to a computer and then other people's computers, and then you're reading about other people's responses on a computer, and nothing has changed in the physical world, even though everything has changed.' He had achieved something, something that felt world-changing. But the world was no different.

It was late. I was exhausted, ready for sleep. A lot had happened that day. I flipped through the pages of notes I'd been scribbling down in my notebook, trying in vain to keep up with everything Craig had been telling me. I could barely read my awful handwriting. I realized I'd need to stay up for a few more hours and transcribe my notes while they were fresh in my memory. By morning, these scratchings would be meaningless. But I wanted to ask one more question.

It seemed a bit like Craig was sweeping *Sworcery* under the carpet. It seemed like he had set up this day's events so that we could deal with *Sworcery* and be done with it. It was like there was something too painful about it – that he would take it like a necessary arrow in his calf, then pull it out, and we could continue. And it wasn't just the way our day was set up: it seemed like that was how he had lived his life post-*Sworcery*. It was as if it needed to be sealed off hermetically so he could move on, jettisoned like garbage before a hyperspace jump.

Yeah, in a way that's how it was, Craig told me. He did feel the need to move on. It was indeed his plan to talk about *Sworcery* today so we wouldn't need to talk about it for the rest of the weekend.

The problem lay with the reaction to the game. Most of it was incredibly positive. The game sold tons of copies, it got lots of reviews. But even the positive reviews missed something crucial about it. It was widely regarded as a 'hipster' game. It seemed ironic, detached, too cool for school. For every comment praising it as an achievement and a step forward for the medium, there were two or three calling it pretentious and up its own ass.

The best reviews understood that the game's cool outside covered a profoundly sincere core. In *Rock, Paper, Shotgun*, Kieron Gillen described *Sworcery*'s 'don't-give-a-fuck-and-nothing-has-ever-made-me-give-a-fuck' attitude as a pose:

> Its insincerity is a mask. It's the most sincere, unironic game I've played in ages. […] It covers it with layers of irony, but it's based on a sincere belief that this shit means something. It could come across as being embarrassed of what it is, except it's more like shyness. As in, what it's talking about is too important to be approached directly and crassly. You have to joke about it, because if you take it seriously, it'll shatter.

Gillen got it, which was great, but that didn't mean everyone agreed. You can see in the comments section of Gillen's review itself. Someone named Hentzau writes, 'I thought *Sword & Sworcery* was complete tripe devoid of anything resembling form, substance, wit or charm, instead relying on a series of tired memes, references and injokes to carry the day.' Crudzilla: 'This game is just pretentious. And that irritates me.'

These sorts of comments grated on Craig and wore him down. Eventually he started to agree with them. He was sick of the loud, assertive, over-the-top persona he'd developed for himself. As Gillen said, it was a pose, but the pose was getting all the attention: it was distracting from what he really wanted to create. It was time to move on: from Toronto, from *Sworcery*, from Superbrothers as it had existed to that point.

There was a fourth folder on the USB stick, mysteriously labelled '04 the future.' This was where he had gathered materials for his next project, a new collaboration with an old friend named Patrick McAllister, whose indie game *nom de guerre* was Pine Scented.

Craig said it was time to go there, into the future.

It's what we'd talk about tomorrow.

4.

I was already up, chatting with Jori in the living room, when Craig woke up at 10 a.m. and made us a breakfast of eggs and mushrooms. Once we'd finished, he made me an Americano and brought me into a room I hadn't been in or even noticed the previous day. Craig was such a careful stage manager. He had clearly wanted to talk about the new project in a new room, free of any antiquated associations from our *Sworcery*-centric conversation of the night before.

This trajectory worried me. He still liked *Sworcery*, right? I mean, I'd come all the way here because I loved *Sworcery*, and because I wanted to see what its creator would do next. Talking to Craig the day before had only made me love it more. All the wild, ambitious, avant-garde things I thought it was trying to do – it was really trying to do all of them! Surely the next game would be even wilder, even more ambitious, even more avant-garde. With all the money he'd made with *Sworcery* – with everything he'd learned, all the people he'd met – he'd be able to do exactly what he wanted this time, on his own terms, in his own way. I was dying to hear about it.

No, Craig told me.

The first description I got of the next project was an avalanche of negations. No pixels. No irony. No hipstery language. No dumb manifestos. No weird indieness for the sake of being indie. No 'indie aesthetic' at all. No posing. Instead, 3D. Sincerity. More of a videogame-videogame, made for a traditional console, not a phone. Videogames as a form of 'exercise' rather than a Marinettian vehicle for social explosion. An evolution of *Fatal Inertia*, in some ways. It was a flying game.

My heart sank.

The new room was a kind of solarium, tucked behind the kitchen. It had a couch, a TV, and a big theatrical poster for *Star Trek IV: The Voyage Home* framed on the wall. My sister had been a dangerously obsessive *Star Trek* fan as a teen – her watch was set to Pacific time so that she would always be able to visualize the daily routines of Brent Spiner, the actor who played Data on *The Next Generation*, who lived in Brentwood, California – and I'd been dragged along to the point that I had all the movies memorized. *The Voyage Home* was the goofy one where the original cast slingshot themselves off the sun and time-travel back to present-day Earth to retrieve a pre-extinction humpback whale and save the future. It was one of my favourites. Craig and I geeked out on *Star Trek* for a while and then moved on to *Star Wars*. That had become my own dangerous obsession in my first year of high school. For whatever reason, I'd avoided making friends that year, and had instead spent most of my evenings and weekends reading horrible spinoff novels (those Timothy Zahn novels where Luke Skywalker fights clones of himself, designated as such by extra U's in their names: Luke, Luuke, Luuuuuuke), collecting terrible comics series, endlessly rewatching my VHS box set of the original theatrical releases of episodes four through six. I remember the deep envy I felt for the people who had never seen these films, because they would still be able to experience them for the first time, have that thrill of fresh discovery, something lost to me forever. It may have been my first experience of nostalgia, the earliest stirrings of adulthood.

I hadn't thought of sci-fi much since high school. It was something that I had consciously put behind me in order to become a somewhat normal teenager with friends and a life. I definitely didn't have time for Zahn-level trash when I was studying Serious Literature during the decade of my B.A.-M.A.-PhD cycle. Like videogames, sci-fi was something I'd outgrown.

Craig felt differently. Over the years, his respect for the genre had only grown, fuelled by his admiration not for its otherworldly escapism but its ability to provide hope and direction in the present. That day, in the Sci-Fi Solarium, he spoke to me in staggering detail and at incredible length about *2001*, *Alien*, *Dark Star*, Antonio Jodorowsky's doomed adaptation of *Dune*, Werner Herzog's *Aguirre, the Wrath of God* and *Lessons of Darkness*. A lot of his interest in them was fan interest: improbable stories, amazing art, cool ships, weird planets. But the main current was a belief in sci-fi's ability to get people to imagine a different life. Not just individually, but collectively: to model different social arrangements, different values, different ethics. *Star Trek* was his favourite example of this. Even the original series, for all its silliness, showed the 1960s what it might be like to live in a world where people of all races and backgrounds worked together for a common goal, governed by stringent moral codes and guided by a faith in science and reason. Craig had just finished reading *My Dream of Stars*, a memoir by Anousheh Ansari, who had paid $20 million to become the first female space tourist. She had spent a week on the International Space Station, her flight patch bearing both the Iranian and US flags at a time of particular tension between the two countries. Craig found the story inspiring, and he was not in the least surprised to learn that Ansari had been an obsessive *Star Trek* fan as a kid in Iran, that that was the origin of her 'dream of stars.'

I bet we spent five hours in that sunny secret room talking about science-fiction. Not a word had been spoken about the game, but I felt a bit like I was being led through the basement of a closed construction site, like when a banker is given a hard hat and allowed to prowl around where they wouldn't normally be permitted. I'd been shown the ideological skeleton of the game, the myths and tropes that its narrative had been built on. Looking back on this now, I wonder if it wasn't also some kind of test. If I could keep up during the tour of the subterranean realms of the game, if I could show that I knew my stuff and had paid my dues in the sci-fi underworld, then I could see the other levels. Maybe if I hadn't memorized the script of *Star Trek IV* – I remember Craig laughing hard when I repeated Spock's immortal line, 'Double dumbass on you' – I wouldn't have been admitted to the next room. But eventually, after lunch, I was – literally. Now, in a new corner of the living room, sitting beneath the wooden stag head gifted him by Jim Guthrie, he began to tell me about what was then called *The Future*.

Basically, it was a game where you fly a little spaceship around a planet. You explore, you encounter creatures, you interact with ecosystems, you listen, you look around, you find things that interest you, you try to survive, you make decisions that affect the creatures you've met, the ecosystem you inhabit, and your own place in that world.

So how do you actually tell the story? He and Patrick had some ideas about this.

You start by subtracting. You want your characters to be relatively blank so that your players can bring them to life, inhabit them with their own experiences and values. You want a minimum of cutscenes – those little quasi-movies that link together playing sequences to tie everything into a coherent narrative. You don't want to 'tell,' or even 'show,' but leave genuine space for players to create meaning in their own way. In this sense, the *Sworcery* manifesto, 'Less Talk, More Rock,' still applied. The narrative, such as it is, unfolds through dialogue, but all the dialogue needs to be optional. You can't force players to sit through conversations with other characters, or block their progress until they've clicked through a massive thread. For it to have an impact, they need to actually want to listen and talk.

So you start with a commitment to giving the player full control over how much of the narrative they actually want to dig into: you're never going to force it down their throats. But that doesn't mean you get to ignore narrative. Even if the player only ends up taking two steps on the 514-kilometre-long road you've created, those two steps will make sense and resonate only if you've imagined every bend along the way, every intersection, every station house, every tree, every bird on every branch. It's Hemingway's iceberg, only in a good videogame you don't get to decide how much of the iceberg the player actually sees, because at any moment they should be allowed to put on their scuba gear and go explore underwater. So you build the whole thing, you imagine everything, and you develop game mechanics that allow your player to dive in exactly as deeply as they want to.

This can all get overwhelming when your game is set in a different universe, focuses on a totally different culture, and takes place over a span of more than a thousand years. You need to imagine entire histories, governing philosophies, scientific systems. But if you can sort out these grand macro-level things, they will seep down into all the micro-level details of the game and give everything a ring of truth. Who are the pilots? What culture formed them? What kinds of ships and equipment would people formed in this culture produce? If a pilot is sitting alone next to a fire and you tap them on the shoulder, what will they say? What will their voice sound like? To have good answers to any of these questions – answers that resonate with the big themes of the game, that connect the micro level to the macro in a seamless chain – you need to have what Craig called 'lore.'

Shigeru Miyamoto, legendary game designer and producer at Nintendo, once said that an idea is something that solves multiple problems at once. 'That's what we're driving toward,' Craig told me. 'I see lore as a tool to sculpt our world, make it cohesive and implicitly meaningful.' I was about to be introduced to *The Future*'s lore.

But before he laid it out, Craig asked me if I wanted another coffee. We got up and went back to the kitchen, and as we stood around the espresso machine, he talked to me a bit more about the way that game mechanics connect to lore.

The *BioShock* series functioned for Craig as a kind of cautionary tale. It was famous for its killer lore. The first two installments, *BioShock* and *BioShock 2*, set in the fictional underwater city of Rapture, were explorations (and, quite transparently, travesties) of Ayn Rand's philosophy of Objectivism, with a bit of George Orwell thrown in. *BioShock Infinite*, set in the floating city of Columbia, makes an ideological assault on the racism and elitism at the heart of American exceptionalism. I remember when I was on the job market in 2015, touring around universities giving talks about digital literature and the future of narrative, *BioShock* was the only game anyone would admit to playing. The professors, I'm sure, genuinely didn't play videogames. But I'm *positive* all the grad students were secretly spending their spare hours on *Animal Crossing* and *Gears of War* – they just wouldn't admit that to a potential future professor.

BioShock was one of the game series I'd given a shot when I was starting to get excited about videogames, around the time *Sworcery* came out. I truly hated it. I downloaded the original *BioShock* and *BioShock Infinite*, all bazillion gigabytes of them, from the App Store, and had been turned off both almost immediately. In the first one, I felt like I was back in *Doom*, gun in hand, stubbly and muscular and troubled in an ex-military kind of way, descending into some scary world where I would have to shoot a bunch of living things. I stopped playing before I had to kill anything and long before I had a chance to delve into the game's argument against Ayn Rand. *BioShock Infinite* held my interest a little longer. I was having fun poking around an early twentieth-century floating carnival, checking out the snack stalls and the hat shops, listening to a barbershop quartet anachronistically crooning the Beach Boys' 'God Only Knows' from a miraculously suspended platform. Then, suddenly, brutally, a gun was forced into my hand, I was shooting people – I had no choice – and there was blood everywhere. That jarring transition between the wonder of the floating city and the horror of dead carnival-goers was the most awful thing I'd experienced in a videogame.

Craig explained this as a failure to connect lore to mechanics. Sure, *BioShock* was informed by a bunch of high concepts inspired by history and religion and philosophy, which is great, and which videogames need. But in its DNA, it's still as dumb as *Doom*: it's a shooter, you run around and kill lots of people. The high-concept lore remains skin-deep – insultingly so – unless you give your players something to do other than shoot stuff. You can't just squish your big ideas into the existing framework of a stupid violent videogame. You need to fundamentally reshape the gameplay to match the idea. One of the goals of The Future was to create an experience where narrative reality and gameplay were one and the same.

Mugs in hand, we returned to sit beneath the stag's head. It was time to be initiated into the lore.

The story of The Future begins with a story. In a world something like our own, with a geography somewhat akin to that of earth, there is a place a bit like the USSR. It is a period a bit like the mid-twentieth century, but different. Rather than being dominated by ethnic Russians and centred in Moscow, this USSR is led by a people reminiscent of Mongolians, who have consolidated their global power over centuries, descendants of a figure like Genghis Khan. This people is the dominant world power – there is no United States to rival them – and they owe their position of global dominance to technological ingenuity. Theirs is a fully industrialized society whose domestic and military machinery is much more advanced than that of any other civilization. But there are two problems. First, this civilization faces imminent ecological disaster. They have industrialized too rapidly and too completely, and they are rendering their world unlivable. Second, evidence has begun to suggest that this civilization's mythic belief in periodic planetary cataclysms – year-long meteor showers that destroy all but the most ingenious and farsighted – is not legend but fact. The next such event is due in the coming centuries.

This double threat has brought renewed prominence to a classic literary work that is beginning to look more and more like non-fiction, like prophecy. Toward the end of a period analogous to our nineteenth century, as the first wave of industrialization was coming to a close, there emerged a writer analogous to Tolstoy: a beloved and towering figure remembered as the greatest artist of his time. His masterpiece is a work that blends traditional legend with science fiction. The first part of this work takes place in the deep past, narrating the civilization's central cultural myth, the story of the female shaman regarded as the nation's founder. She foresees the first of the planetary cataclysms and, shunned for her unorthodox beliefs, nonetheless succeeds in surviving the apocalypse, sheltering herself and her adherents by tunnelling into a massive, symmetrical mountain, where they live for a full year. The lessons drawn from the shaman's tale are fearlessness, iconoclasm, ingenuity, and the importance of careful observation: she and her people survive because they noticed the celestial portents, overthrew traditional beliefs in responding to imminent threat, and intelligently harvested the plants and resources necessary to survive underground.

The second part of the Tolstoy figure's book takes place in the distant future, on a different planet. The shaman's descendants, colonists dispatched from the USSR-like civilization, are living in a settlement whose landscape is dominated by a huge, symmetrical mountain, an echo of the mountain where their civilization took root. They have been called to this distant planet by a signal – a transmission across far reaches of space and time, carried deep into their civilization's collective unconscious. For centuries these people had dreamed every night of a mountain on a far-distant planet, a shelter to which their civilization could escape before the next meteor shower, predicted to be so powerful that it would destroy their planet completely. Impelled by their dreams, they build equipment that detects an actual radio signal originating from an eons-distant planet. They build ships to reach it, and eventually live there in peace.

Most read the work of this Tolstoy figure as fiction, but others treat it as fact. They too are haunted by dreams of a distant mountain, huge and symmetrical, signalling life and survival. As the society's technology advances, as radio telescopes develop, they are the ones who first hear it: the signal, an uncanny pattern, uninterpretable but unquestionably meaningful, impossible to dismiss as noise. As in the fictional work, in the real life of this civilization, the mythic signal turns out to be real. As telescopes develop, they reveal the source of the signal: a planet, with an atmosphere and ocean, regulated by life. With the threat of cataclysm and ecological disaster upon them, this civilization unites to send colonists to the planet. It takes decades, or hundreds of years, but they succeed in building the ships and training the pilots to undertake this mission. The crew is placed in suspended animation and, after a thousand-year journey, awake to find themselves orbiting the planet.

The story as a whole was called *The Future*. The first slice of it, which Craig was already working on, told the story of the initial contact with the new planet. It was called *The Far Shore*.

That, at least, is the brutally simplified version of it, as best as I can remember it. It took Craig hours to talk me through all this – it was pitch black by the time he finished. He couldn't mention the name Genghis Khan, for instance, without getting up and taking his Khan biography off the shelf, telling me about the salient points in his life, all the reasons Craig respected his craftiness and survival skills, all the ways that world history would have been different if he'd managed to seed a genuinely dominant global civilization. It was a magnificent performance. Inevitably, my account above will sound cheesy and clichéd and uncomfortably like the Wikipedia plot summary of blandly by-the-book sci-fi. You will have to trust me that in the moment it was mesmerizing, even for a thoroughly cynical, done-with-sci-fi person like myself. Craig had been reading and dreaming and imagining this world, clearly, for many years. He was totally possessed by it. For a few thrilling hours, he laid it all out before me, in such overwhelming detail and massive scope that I was unable to take notes, or take it all in, but just let it hit me like a rogue wave.

Part of the appeal, too, was that Craig seemed to have some kind of role in mind for me in all this. I wasn't there just to listen. I wasn't there just to make notes that would someday turn into a book that would serve as a marketing device or give the game a scholarly sheen. Craig repeatedly paused to solicit my advice and input. It was quite clear, for instance, that he thought I knew a lot about Tolstoy, and that this knowledge of mine would allow him to nail down his thinking about this all-important writer-figure, eventually known as Tsosi. Well, I had read *War and Peace* a few times, and *Anna Karenina* a few more. I had read Nabokov praise Tolstoy and Bakhtin trash him. But I was really just a fan. My PhD was in twentieth-century British literature: Tolstoy was from the wrong country and century. I remember saying, at one point, 'You do know Tolstoy never wrote any science-fiction, right?' That was about the limit of my usefulness.

That didn't seem to diminish Craig's faith in my abilities, somehow. I could see, in his intense and earnest eyes, that he believed in me – believed that I could bring something to this project, some kind of intellectual ballast, some kind of shamanic wisdom. The thrill of this stayed with me for the rest of the weekend. It stayed with me that night, when he showed me the stingy, scraggly, clunky demo of a tiny, pixellated ship flying across a roughly coloured landscape, with characters sliding into ships like chess pieces. It stayed with me through a long bus ride back from Magog to Montreal. Walking toward the Gare Centrale to catch my train back to Toronto, I stopped at a Tim Horton's, which I knew had free wi-fi, and wrote Craig an email on my iPhone 3GS:

Thanks again to you and Jori for being such amazing hosts. I'm really excited about the book and *The Future* and the future!

To bury my earnestness a little, I added another line:

I'm pretty sure I forgot my travel shampoo thing in your shower, btw. No big loss!

PART II

MODERNISM COMES TO THE VIDEOGAME

5.

In the winter of 2014, I was sitting in my living room, carefully positioned in front of my photogenic bookshelf, doing a Skype interview for a job at San Diego State University that I was sure I wasn't going to get. I was so sure I wasn't going to get it that when they asked me a very standard interview question – What would be your dream course to teach? – I skipped my usual tactic of giving them my best guess at what I thought *their* dream course would be. I told them about my actual dream course.

It would be about the history of independent art. It wouldn't fit into any one discipline or historical period. It would be about independent writing, music, and videogames, all together: self-published magazines in 1910, DIY presses in the twenties, mimeographed chapbooks in the fifties, self-financed punk shows in the seventies, indie labels in the eighties, photocopied zines in the nineties – and indie games today. It would be about the connections between all these forms – about the way that socially progressive movements in the arts seem to emerge only when it becomes possible to do it yourself, when new technologies and new ways of using them coincide to allow anyone to say whatever they want on their own terms without having to get anyone else's approval.

I didn't think much more about this course – which in my mind was perfect but also impossible: too weird, too many forms of art all squashed together, too many time periods – until, against all expectations, I got the job, moved to San Diego, and filled out a form about what courses I was interested in teaching for the upcoming semester. I got an email from the department chair: 'What about that indie course?'

In waking life, my dream course became known as Comparative Literature 594, 'The Social Politics of Indie.' I hadn't known what to expect from it – and most of all, I hadn't known who would sign up. Walking around campus, everyone I saw seemed so happy and tanned, riding their hoverboards from building to building, every last one of them in a San Diego State University hoodie. These didn't seem like the sorts of kids who cared about punk zines. But my class had drawn out the weirdos.

By the midpoint in the semester, the students and I had bonded over Patti Smith, X-Ray Spex, riot grrrl, and Virginia Woolf – our connection all the closer because of how cut off we all felt from the SDSU norm. One day, we were about to play our first indie videogame, *Gone Home*. The entire semester had been building up to this moment. *Gone Home* fulfills pretty much all the fantasies of indie development. It was made by a small team living in a rented house in, of course, Portland. When you first start playing the game, you think you're in another first-person shooter: you play as Katie Greenbriar, who returns from a summer abroad to find her family home – massive, Victorian, slightly decaying, a textbook haunted house – abandoned. At first you think monsters are going to jump out at you, but eventually you see that there's no one to fight, just a story to uncover. As you walk around, pick up objects, read notes, and listen to tapes, you find yourself immersed in a queer narrative: your parents are away at couples therapy, and your little sister Samantha – discriminated against at school and at home – has taken the opportunity to run away with her girlfriend.

I loved a lot of things about the game, but what I loved most was the way it tied itself to the history of independent art. The tapes you pick up and listen to are all from the early-nineties riot grrrl movement – bands like Bratmobile and Heavens to Betsy, whose politically charged music was released on tiny indie labels. Riot grrrl bands didn't just make and release music independently, they also made their own photocopied zines (Allison Wolfe and Molly Neuman from Bratmobile founded *Girl Germs*, one of the first riot grrrl zines, and co-founded *riot grrrl* itself, the zine that gave the movement its name). As you wander around the family mansion, you eventually find a hidden room where Samantha has made a zine of her own, *Kicking Against the Patriarchy*. The room itself is a kind of diorama tribute to the DIY ideals of punk – walls covered in posters for local shows; desks covered with the bits of paper, scissors, and markers that Samantha and her girlfriend used to make the zines; floors lined with stacks of the zines, ready for distribution. It was also a perfect example of Virginia Woolf's 'room of one's own': a space away from power in which historically disenfranchised people could create whatever they wanted in their own way.

Gone Home was supposed to be the climax of the course. We'd read Virginia Woolf's *A Room of One's Own* and Allison Wolfe's *Girl Germs*, we'd listened to Bratmobile and Heavens to Betsy, we'd studied Kill Rock Stars, the independent label from Olympia, Washington, that released their music – in part *because* they were referenced in *Gone Home*, in part *because* of the pleasure I'd have in seeing the lightbulbs go off as the students realized that culture is coherent, that movements are linked, that indie games weren't the radically new movement that so many press accounts wanted us to believe they were, but just the latest expression of the same attitude and inclination that produced modernist literature and punk rock.

But things didn't go that way at all. As I started the lecture, giving my usual setup with artist bios and an account of the backstory, I could feel something was off in the room. When I showed a picture of two of the creators of *Gone Home*, Steve Gaynor and Carla Zimonja, dressed in full-on punk regalia, I heard someone mutter, 'stupid hipsters.' The giggles echoed. When I'd finished my setup, I closed my PowerPoint window and switched to the Steam app. As my cursor circled in on the green 'Play' button, all forty voices in the room spoke up in unison: 'NO!'

It took me a while to figure out what was happening. 'NO' what? Did I have the wrong window mirrored on the projector? Was I clicking on the wrong thing? Was I in some sort of danger?

I asked them what was up. A brave student, speaking for the class, said, 'Please, don't make us see any more of that game. It's horrible.'

Never in my life, in all the courses I'd ever taught, had the students rebelled against the selection of a text on my syllabus. Maybe they'd complained among themselves, but they never banded together to refuse – to claim the power to decide what they would read and what was out of bounds. These students did so with absolute assurance, with total confidence that they were right and I was wrong: that this was a bad game, and we would not be looking at it together. This experience taught me several things. Videogames don't belong to the professors, they belong to the students. My reasons for loving *Gone Home* were perhaps my own, and those of a professor. If indie games are a repetition of literary modernism or punk culture, they are repetition with a difference.

Perhaps I should back up here. Leaving aside video games, the connection between modernist literature and punk culture might not be immediately obvious to everyone. It certainly wasn't to me. That started to change when, roughly about the same time I first came across *Sworcery*, I happened to be developing a deep obsession with British post-punk: Throbbing Gristle, Orange Juice, that kind of thing. This obsession led me to Simon Reynolds' history of the genre, *Rip It Up and Start Again: Postpunk 1978–1984*, and a passage that blew my mind:

> Those postpunk years from 1978 to 1984 saw the systematic ransacking of twentieth-century modernist art and literature. The entire postpunk period looks like an attempt to replay virtually every major modernist theme and technique via the medium of pop music. Cabaret Voltaire took their name from Dada. Pere Ubu took theirs from Alfred Jarry. Talking Heads turned a Hugo Ball sound poem into a tribal-disco dance track. Gang of Four, inspired by Brecht and Godard's alienation effects, tried to deconstruct rock even as they rocked hard. […] This frenzied looting of the

archives of modernism culminated with the founding of renegade pop label ZTT – short for Zang Tuum Tumb, a snatch of Italian futurist prose-poetry – and their conceptual group the Art of Noise, named in homage to Luigi Russolo's manifesto for a futurist music.

Taking the word 'modernist' in a less specific sense, the postpunk bands were firmly committed to the idea of making modern music. They were totally confident that there were still places to go with rock, a whole new future to invent. For the postpunk vanguard, punk had failed because it attempted to overthrow rock's status quo using conventional music (fifties rock n' roll, garage punk, mod) that actually predated dinosaur megabands like Pink Floyd and Led Zeppelin. The postpunks set forth with the belief that 'radical content demands radical form.'

Though I had done a PhD in modernist literature and spent my youth in punk bands, I had always thought of them as separate things. Modernism was something that happened at the start of the twentieth century, in the wake of Nietzsche's Death of God and in the midst of two catastrophic world wars. Punk and its offshoots were likewise highly localized affairs: urban decay on the Lower East Side, the Jubilee, Thatcher.

What Reynolds made me see was that they were the same thing played out in different artistic mediums. Everything that excited me about modernist literature and art – abstraction, angularity, daring weirdness, confrontation, rejection of tradition, difficulty, the active attention they demanded of the audience – was also present in punk and (especially) post-punk. And just as all this was revolutionarily new in literature and art in the early twentieth century, what the punks were doing was also absolutely new in pop music in the late seventies/early eighties. Sure, there were Schoenberg and Strauss and Debussy in classical music, but that wasn't a popular form. And one of the reasons modernism was always so exciting to me was that people noticed it.

In the early twentieth century, literature was the dominant popular art form, and the lines between 'high' literary fiction and 'low' popular forms weren't well defined or tightly policed, so that when Virginia Woolf or James Joyce wrote in a new way, people were paying enough attention to be outraged. The excitement of punk was that it entered the arena of popular music and did everything that modernism did for literature and art. Punk was the modernist phase of popular music. What Reynolds' passage taught me was that modernism wasn't some fixed moment in time – 1880–1950, 1914–1945, 1922, whatever – but was instead a stage of development that every art form passes through in its own time. Modernism came to literature and art in the early 1900s. It came to pop music in the late seventies. It had come to jazz even earlier.

Reynolds was not the first to outline this kind of transhistorical version of modernism, and I was not the first to be blown away by it. In his book *All What Jazz*, English poet Philip Larkin, who wrote a music column for the *Daily Telegraph* from 1961 to 1971, explains how his disdain for what was then 'modern jazz' crystallized while reading some contemporary criticism:

> There was something about the books I was now reading that seemed oddly familiar. This *development*, this *progress*, this *new* language that was more *difficult*, more *complex*, that required you to *work hard at appreciating it*, that you *couldn't expect to understand at first go*, that needed *technical and professional knowledge* to evaluate it at *all* levels, this *revolutionary explosion* that *spoke for our time* while at the same time being *traditional* in the *fullest*, the *deepest* … Of course! This was the language of criticism of modern painting, modern poetry, modern music. *Of course!* How glibly I had talked of modern jazz, without realizing the force of the adjective: this was *modern* jazz, and Parker was a modern jazz player just as Picasso was a modern painter and Pound a modern poet. I hadn't realized that jazz had gone from Lascaux to

Jackson Pollock in fifty years, but now I realized it, and relief came flooding in upon me after nearly two years' despondency. I went back to my books: 'After Parker, you had to be something of a musician to follow the best jazz of the day.' Of course! After Picasso! After Pound! There could hardly have been a conciser summary of what I don't believe about art.

The adjective had been there all along. But, as I did, Larkin needed some prodding to see the connection, that modern jazz – Parker, Mingus, Coleman, Coltrane – was *modernist jazz*, the daring, experimental, confrontational phase of that particular form of art.

Modernism comes to different forms at different times. It had come to literature, to painting, to jazz, to pop music. Was it now coming to the videogame? Ezra Pound, Pablo Picasso, Charlie Parker … Craig D. Adams?

A further question has obsessed me in the years since. If 'modern jazz' is modernism come to jazz, if post-punk is modernism come to pop, if indie games are modernism come to the videogame – why the delay? Of course, videogames didn't exist yet in 1900, and pop music barely did, either. But why did post-punk and indie games crystallize exactly when they did? What was it about 1977 or 2006 specifically – why not 1967 or 1995?

I gradually came up with a theory. Perhaps modernism only 'comes' to a particular art form when it is possible for artists in that form to produce and distribute their work independently. That became possible in art and literature in the early twentieth century, when new technologies made printing cheaper and easier, so they had their modernist phases then. Lowered costs of pressing vinyl and innovations in distribution preceded the formation of the independent labels that underwrote modern jazz in the fifties and sixties (Charles Mingus had his own label, Candid Records, on which he released his aptly titled *Charles Mingus Presents Charles Mingus* in 1960) and punk and post-punk in the seventies and eighties – so they had their modernist phases then. Easy-to-use (or at least *easier*-to-use) game engines like Unity, GameMaker, and Twine, along with the emergence of accessible online distribution platforms like Steam and the App Store, allowed the indie/DIY videogame revolution to take place. I've been testing that theory ever since, in academic articles, in this book, in classes like the one I taught in San Diego, and, most recently, in a grad class I taught when I returned to the University of Toronto, called 'Duplicators: the DIY Ethic and DIY Aesthetics in 20th and 21st Century Literature.'

In the first session of that U of T class, I laid out the general contours of my theory – much as I have just done here – and explained to the members of the seminar that our goal for the rest of the semester would be not to prove but to *test* this theory. Looking at various DIY movements in literature – Virginia Woolf's Hogarth Press in 1920s England, samizdat in the Soviet Union, riot grrrl in the Seattle/Olympia scene of the 1990s, Twine games today, etc. – we would ask whether my idea made sense, whether a game like *Gone Home* really had more in common with *A Room of One's Own* and *Girl Germs* than it did with *Gears of War* and *BioShock*.

To do that, we would need to define our key terms. First, what is 'the DIY ethic'? It is an attitude, a way of thinking that leads to a way of making art. It is a principled, intentional belief in the artistic and political necessity of working outside of conventional, commercial modes of production. It is a 'materialist ideology' – that is, it is political, and its politics are rooted in practical concerns. The DIY ethic responds to the very vague question 'How can you work honestly and without compromise' in a totally grounded way: by personally controlling the production and distribution of your own works. (This is equally true of the conscious and unconscious mind: even if you *think* you can say what you really mean while working for someone else – express yourself with perfect honesty and total daring despite your contract with BMG or your book deal with Simon and Schuster – you're fooling yourself.) In this DIY ethic, artistic production is motivated not by profit but by a sense of urgency in the transmission of ideas and values – transformative, world-changing ideas. For this reason, DIY works of art are priced as cheaply as possible or given away for free.

And what is a 'duplicator'? It is any technology that makes it possible for an artist to work according to the DIY ethic. For the most part, these technologies are not designed specifically for the production of DIY art, or for art at all. They're often old technologies – forgotten, abandoned machines that creative people have picked up and appropriated for their own purposes, to achieve their desired effect: reproducing their artistic works as cheaply and as rapidly as possible. For this reason, the machine is never enough: it needs to be supplemented by *practices of duplication*, strategies for identifying, gaining access to, and exploiting these machines.

I provided an example from my own adolescence to illustrate the terms. When I was in high school, my friends and I loved writing and felt like we had a lot to say, so it would have made sense for us to write for the school newspaper. But we considered it hopelessly uncool, mostly because there were teachers on the editorial board and everything needed to pass by them for approval. Obviously in the school newspaper you couldn't write about any of the things that mattered to us: sex, drinking, drugs, and skateboarding. Because we knew that, and because we thought all the things we cared about were really important, we decided to start our own newspaper. We had the DIY ethic. The next thing we needed was a duplicator. We weren't about to invent some new machine to make a copy of our paper for every student at our high school. So we looked around for something we could use. As it happened, one kid's dad worked in an office with a photocopier. That was the duplicator. He stole the key to the office, we snuck in at night and stayed up making hundreds of copies and stapling them together, then arrived at school early the next morning and dropped them off in the cafeteria when no one was looking. Those were the practices of duplication.

This being a graduate class, some exploration of duplication and DIY in the language of French theory was in order, and so in the next class we turned to the ideas of Pierre Bourdieu and Jacques Rancière.

Bourdieu provided us with something to argue against – a model of artistic production that didn't make room for DIY art, a model that DIY art seemed to break. For Bourdieu, artistic production is a game – and, like any game, it has rules and goals. What is strange about the game of art, though, is that there are two completely different ways of playing it. On the one hand, popular art works like most other industries. The goal is money, which comes in the form of sales. The feedback system of commercial art is very straightforward: if you're moving lots of units, if lots of people are buying your novels or films, you're doing well, and you keep doing more of what you're doing. In 'high' art, though – you can also call it *real* art, or just *art* – the economic model is exactly reversed, turned upside down. 'Serious' art is just as much of a game as commercial art, but the rules, goals, and feedback system are all different. What serious artists want is not money but prestige. In their world, sales are actually a counter-indicator of success: real art shouldn't sell, shouldn't reach a wide audience, shouldn't make its creator millions, because all of that would indicate compromise, conformity, playing along, when real artists acquire their prestige by being rebellious, ahead of their time, intransigent, stubborn, unassimilable. If you had set out to be a serious artist and then found that your work had become a best-seller, you would – according to the game logic of high art – have to radically transform your artistic practice, try harder next time to achieve your goal of failure in market ('fail better,' in Samuel Beckett's viral phrase), which would in turn net you more prestige, which was what you were after.

My proposal to the class was that DIY art didn't fit into this model. The reason for this was very practical. If you have a duplicator, your marginal cost – the costs to produce another copy of your book or album or painting – is negligible, a few cents if you had to use the copy shop, zero if you could sneak into your friend's dad's office. These negligible marginal costs fundamentally transform the rules of the game. They do so by removing profit from the equation. If it doesn't cost anything to make another copy, it means you don't have to think about ways of recouping costs or investments, and it means you don't need to charge anything for the stuff you produce. If you're not charging anything for it, you're not seeking profit, and not thinking about art as a commodity in any sense – whether consciously or unconsciously. Duplicators, in other words, make it possible to do something that Bourdieu's model posits as impossible: to play a version of the artistic game in which reaching a wide audience is no longer attached to making money. With DIY, your work can be popular without being commercial. Indeed, it *has* to be popular, and it *has* to be *anti*-commercial. Popular, because how can you change the world without reaching a huge audience? And anti-commercial, because how can you shake the foundations of society while also participating in it, chasing profits like everyone else?

Bourdieu supplied our class with another crucial idea for unpacking the significance of DIY art. For him, the question of what counts as 'art' is incredibly open-ended, flexible, malleable, up for discussion. What the word 'art' refers to is never a given. As such, every artist has to struggle to get their stuff accepted as art. As Bourdieu puts it in *The Field of Cultural Production*, 'The production of discourse about a work of art is part of the production of a work of art.' This isn't a sideshow for Bourdieu, something artists do when they have the time: it's arguably the most important part of any artist's work. If you wanted to go a little further with it, you could say that the artist's fundamental activity – the thing that makes them an artist – is not 'creating beautiful things' or 'telling uncomfortable truths' or whatever. No, for Bourdieu, the artist's fundamental activity is the struggle to enforce a definition of art that fits their work.

This idea helps underline the significance of DIY. To have any chance in the struggle to have your work accepted as art, you need a platform – you need to be able to have your voice heard. If only the rich are writing literature, and if printing books is so incredibly expensive that only rich people own presses, and these presses print only the kind of stuff that aligns with their views, of course the struggle to define art will be quite bland and predictable. But if everyone can publish their work, if anyone's voice can be heard, then the struggle gets much more interesting, and the meaning of 'art' inevitably shifts. As Bourdieu puts it, 'The established definition of the writer may be radically transformed by an enlargement of the set of people who have a legitimate voice in literary matters.' That's exactly what cheap publishing did for literature: radically enlarged the set of people who had – or just claimed – a legitimate voice in literary matters. The result was modernism. By this logic, it stands to reason that game engines like Unity and Twine, by radically enlarging the set of people who are able to claim a legitimate voice in gaming, would lead to a massive rethinking of what games are, and whether they are 'art.' Which is precisely what happened with indie games.

From Jacques Rancière's *The Politics of Aesthetics* we took a vision of why this all matters. Rancière argues that without art we wouldn't see the world. Art provides the mental framework, the cognitive models, to turn a mess of sensory impressions into something coherent and knowable. Artists show us the world, and they provide us with the language for speaking about it – and those two things are directly related, since we don't really see the world until we have the language to talk about it. By doing so, artists provide the groundwork for living and taking action in the world. As he puts it in a lovely turn of phrase, artists 'draft maps of the visible, trajectories between the visible and sayable, relationships between modes of being, modes of saying, and modes of doing and making.'

This, for Rancière, is why art is so important for democracy – or why democracy is only possible with the help of art. In the past – from the beginnings of literary history to the time of the French

Revolution – the role of art was didactic, to craft a shared ethos for a homogeneous community, or to police the borders between what was acceptable behaviour befitting nobles and what was unacceptable, befitting the lower orders. In a democratic age – which Rancière hopefully believes us still to be living in today – art rejects all standards of decorum, represents everything it can get its hands on, rejects all hierarchies of 'high' and 'low,' brings honour to the commonplace. The social role of this kind of art is to extend what Rancière calls 'the distribution of the sensible,' to make things newly visible and sayable, and thus doable and makeable.

DIY and duplication should fit into this narrative in obvious ways. Who better to expand the distribution of the sensible than the people who had been invisible in the older modes of art – the people whose ideas, opinions, class, race, gender, sexual orientation, age, etc., put them squarely in the realm of the unacceptable, the invisible, the unsayable? And what better way to give these people a voice, to give them a say in the expansion of the sayable, than through cheap and accessible technologies and techniques of reproduction?

Rancière also provides a simple way to test whether DIY art is living up to its promise. If it isn't expanding the distribution of the sensible, what's the point?

The rest of the course – ten more weeks of it – looked at a series of examples from literary history to test my theory: to see whether DIY art really upset Bourdieu's model and ask whether any DIY movement really lives up to the Rancière Test. Two case studies were especially insightful: the ones I've already mentioned, Virginia Woolf's Hogarth Press and the riot grrrl movement.

Woolf's book *Three Guineas* – a work of non-fiction first published in 1938 – is amazing in lots of ways. First and foremost, its argument is shockingly badass in its context. On the eve of the Second World War, Woolf argues that fascism isn't 'out there,' across the channel, on the continent. Patriarchy is fascism, she argues – and so fascism is already in Britain, in the family, in education, in the professions, all over the empire, everywhere. The book caused all kinds of outrage, and even upset some of Woolf's friends. So how could she have published it at all – who would have wanted to print an 'anti-British' tract like this with the country about to head into battle? The answer was the Hogarth Press, the publishing house that Woolf herself set up with her husband, Leonard, in 1917 as a hobby, but which by 1938 was a major enterprise.

Fittingly, given all this, *Three Guineas* is also remarkable for containing the earliest formulation of the DIY ethic I've ever come across. If you've read Woolf, you'll know how complicated she can be. Her essays especially are known for making one point, then arguing the exact opposite point for a while, then shifting back and forth before leaving you a bit confused about what exactly she was trying to say. But her arguments about self-publishing in *Three Guineas* are different. They stand out for their absolute clarity. Woolf argues in the essay that every artist should aspire to 'intellectual liberty,' 'the right to say or write what you think in your own words, and in your own way.' If you're writing for money, for an editor, for a publisher, she says, you don't have intellectual liberty. A journalist is 'in the pay of an editor, who is in the pay of a board, which has a policy to pursue.' All writing for pay is compromised; she calls it 'prostitution of the mind.' If you wanted to know what a writer actually meant or believed, you'd have to somehow 'strip each statement of its power motive, of its advertisement motive, of its publicity motive, of its vanity motive' – an impossible task. The way out of this trap is self-publication. In a passage from *Three Guineas* that I have cited endless times and that has had an even greater impact on my intellectual life than the one from *Rip It Up and Start Again*, Woolf writes,

> The private printing press is an actual fact, and not beyond the reach of a moderate income. Typewriters and duplicators are actual facts and even cheaper. By using these cheap and so far unforbidden instruments you can

at once rid yourself of the pressure of boards, policies and editors. They will speak your own mind, in your own words, at your own time, at your own length, at your own bidding. And that, we are agreed, is our definition of 'intellectual liberty.'

How do you achieve intellectual liberty? Woolf's answer is very direct: 'Fling leaflets down basements; expose them on stalls; trundle them along streets on barrows to be sold for a penny or given away.'

The question of whether Woolf practised what she preached is slightly more complicated, and was the source of much debate in class. From one perspective, yes, of course she did. She ran her own press, she was able to publish whatever she liked. Running her own press clearly transformed her writing, too – she only really became 'Virginia Woolf' once she was able to speak her own mind, in her own words, in her own time, at her own length, at her own bidding. It's fitting that the last of her books to be published commercially is called *Night and Day*, because that's how drastic the difference in style is compared with her first self-published book, *Jacob's Room*, which came out only three years later. The fact that her first two novels were published by a firm run by her half-brother, Gerald Duckworth, who had sexually abused her as a child, only intensifies the sense of freedom that entered Woolf's writing after she started Hogarth.

The complications in Woolf's formulation of the DIY ethic come not from any wrinkle in the argument of *Three Guineas* but from her own practices as the owner of Hogarth Press. In short, she made money from it. Hogarth was profitable. And she wouldn't have been able to start it, and it wouldn't have become such a success, if she wasn't from a privileged background and wasn't so well-connected to the conventionally powerful. For the students in the 'Duplicators' class, this took a lot of the shine off the Hogarth Press story. Sure, at various points the Woolfs framed their enterprise in heroic terms: Leonard said they looked to print works 'which would have little or no chance of being published by ordinary publishers.' Virginia spoke of how 'amusing' it was 'to be able to do what one likes – no editors, or publishers.' But – 'amusing'? How serious were they about changing the world? When they initially founded the press, it was for non-ideological reasons: they looked at it as a form of therapy, distraction, and play. Their print runs were relatively small, the readership relatively limited. Hogarth books had such an impact not because they reached a wide audience but because the small audience they reached was made up of the influential, the tastemakers, the elite.

And although, looking back on the founding press on its fifth anniversary, Leonard Woolf boasted that they 'were resolved to produce no book *merely* with a view to pecuniary profit,' that didn't mean they were opposed to profit if a book happened to sell well. Hogarth was a meticulously run business, profitable from its first book. They never gave books away for free, and they did not share profits equally with their authors, even if these authors were badly off. Can you still call yourself DIY if you're making money? Or if you're speaking only to the elite? For many students in the class, the answer was a definite no, and so *nothing* was ever fully satisfying. There was always some little trace of impurity, some example of less-than-perfect magnanimity, some schism between what was preached and what was practised, that would make every self-proclaimed DIYer feel like a bit of a hypocrite.

Riot grrrl was another case in point. In most ways, the movement shows everything that is best, most hopeful, most socially transformative about DIY culture. It started as a response to the failed idealism of punk: where punk promised an alliance of the outcasts, a wholesale rejection of mainstream culture carried out by a bloc of freaks, in practice it could be just as exclusionary as the society it opposed. In particular, it was violent, masculinist, sexist. Being a teenage girl at a punk show could be frightening, dangerous, and alienating. Riot grrrl was about reclaiming and reinventing punk. It used the tools that punk had developed – the music, the clothes, the shows, the communities, the methods of publication and distribution – to achieve something bigger than just letting white suburban boys express their frustration.

What we focused on in our class were the riot grrrl zines: *Jigsaw, Chainsaw, riot grrrl, Bikini Kill, Girl Germs, Gunk, I'm So Fucking Beautiful*. These checked all the boxes for the DIY ethic. They were made for next to nothing, photocopied and given away or sold for pennies at shows – no profits were made. There were no editors or publishers involved, no one but writers and readers. The aesthetic was purposefully and delightfully messy – typos and handwritten corrections all over the place. Zinesters talked about how anyone could make a zine or start a band or make a record, and looking at their proudly amateurish productions showed you that this was true. The zines were also girly and un-masculine, with hearts and stars filling all empty space. And they clearly passed the Rancière Test. They extended the distribution of the sensible to include the perspective and the voices of teenage girls, talking in an unfiltered way about the things that mattered to them. There were articles about TV, about fights with friends, about whatever was pissing them off at the moment; there were also totally taboo pieces on violence, incest, and rape. Riot grrrl zines gave a language to a whole sphere of existence that had seldom or never been expressed.

But just as riot grrrl called punk on its failure to live up to its ideals, others have called riot grrrl on failing to live up to its own. There were some limitations to its viewpoint. Most of the canonical riot grrrl zines were made by a few people, a group of friends – most of whom happened to be white, straight, cis, and middle-class. People of colour, trans people, LGBTQ people, working-class people – they all struggled to find a place in riot grrrl, even as they were drawn to its message and its methods. Riot grrrl promised inclusion, promised that readers could become authors, that anyone could do it – but it turned out that it wasn't that simple, and that all the usual categories of oppression still applied.

A recurrent debate in the class was whether DIY really existed. It seemed there was always some flaw, some impurity, some partially realized aim, that got in the way. Some students in the Duplicators class decided that the way out of this was to treat the DIY ethic not as an absolute but as aspirational – something you could, at best, approach asymptotically but never reach. That was enough: trying was much better than not trying, being 80 percent good was better than 100 percent evil. You could achieve a lot without achieving everything.

In the months after the class ended, I tried to work out a new definition of DIY. Okay, so DIY movements always turn out to be impure. What if we embraced impurity as a defining trait of DIY?

Bourdieu proposed two models of artistic production: one that sought maximum reach and maximum profit; one that sought minimum reach and maximum prestige. DIY art is neither: it seeks maximum reach and takes social transformation as its goal, not prestige or money. Bourdieu's model is binary: you're either one or the other. DIY breaks the binary, and is in that sense inherently impure. It is impure at birth – in the language of my academic discipline, it is always-already impure.

Maybe that's a way out of all these discussions about the failures of DIY. DIY exists in the spaces where Bourdieu's model breaks down, where it gets messy. Looked at in this way, we shouldn't be surprised by its messiness. If anything, we should insist on the messiness of DIY. Messiness is what DIY is.

I'm still not sure I'm convinced by this messiness business. But it's certainly appropriate for the game that had come, by the time I was working out these theories, to be known to the world as JETT: *The Far Shore*.

6.

If this book had come out in 2015 or 2016, as initially planned, it would have been one of the first about indie games. But it didn't, and in the interim other books came along, most notably, Jesper Juul's *Handmade Pixels: Independent Video Games and the Quest for Authenticity*, published by MIT Press in 2019. Juul's starting point is defamiliarization. As one of the pioneers of the academic study of videogames – he had an important article in the inaugural issue of the journal *Game Studies* in 2001, and his seminal book *Half-Real* came out in 2005 – what strikes Juul most about indie games is how new they feel. The opening words of *Handmade Pixels* are, 'It was as if someone pressed the RESET button.' Though he had spent much of his life 'playing and writing about video games,' indie games gave him 'the refreshing feeling of starting over, of once again *not knowing what video games are* and having to discover them from the beginning':

> I came to independent video games because I was tired of video games about running through hallways shooting things, because I was fascinated with the underdog, entranced by radical new ideas of what games could be, enmeshed in lively gatherings and late-night discussions about a new video game, grown bottom-up outside the shackles of big corporations and expressing new ideas and personal experiences.

He takes as the subject of his book 'strange new games and the conflicts around them.'

Of course, as a distinguished academic writing the first book about indie games for a major academic press, Juul can't allow himself to luxuriate for very long in this realm of strangeness, conflict, uncertainty, and defamiliarization. The principal aim of *Handmade Pixels* is to define indie games – to get a handle on them, to make sense of them, to make them knowable. But it's a difficult task, and Juul is forced to approach it from many angles, none of which lead to easy answers. The first problem is that the 'independence' of indie games can take many forms and mean many things. He distinguishes between three types of independence: financial, aesthetic, and cultural. Financial independence means you didn't take anyone else's money to make your game, so you weren't burdened by the compromises – conscious or unconscious – that this entails. Aesthetic independence means that your game stands out as stylistically different from 'normal' or 'mainstream' games, jarring or strange or unfamiliar in terms of its design. Cultural independence means that your game stands apart not only from mainstream games, but also from mainstream culture writ large, standing in opposition to it and seeking to change it. As Juul writes, a culturally independent game carries a 'cultural, political, and moral promise' – a faith that it can 'make the world a better place.'

Juul notes that what counts as 'indie' has shifted between these three categories throughout the genre's brief history, sometimes in overlapping, contradictory, incoherent combinations. He demonstrates this by tracking the shifting entry criteria for the Independent Games Festival, the annual gathering of indie developers that has been essential to bringing recognition to the movement, and which brought *Sworcery* its first industry attention. At the inaugural IGF in 1999, independence was strictly defined in terms of financial independence: the rules of entry specified that games 'developed, financed, or in any way assisted by a Commercial Publisher' would be 'deemed ineligible for the Festival and [...] disqualified.' (Whether the IGF itself could be considered 'indie' in these terms is very much in doubt: it takes place within the Game Developers Conference, the commercial videogame industry's major conference.) By 2007, the IGF was faced with a flood of games that occupied a nebulous region: developed by small studios that were 'commercial' in the sense of being operated for profit, but which were minuscule compared to the behemoths that dominated the industry. It thus revised its entry requirements: an 'Ineligible Publisher' was now any member of the 'Entertainment Software Association (ESA) and/or the Entertainment and Leisure Software Publishers Association (ELSPA),' of which the behemoths were all members. By the next year, however, any attempt to police a definition of independence in financial terms had been abandoned. The 2008 IGF offered a vague definition that mixed the financial, the aesthetic, and the cultural: as long as a game was 'created in the "indie spirit"' and as long as its creator felt like an 'independent developer' – 'an artistically independent game creator making the kinds of games that [they] want[ed] to make' – they were welcome. It was a non-definition on par with Justice Stewart's 'I know it when I see it' rule for pornography – effectively an admission of defeat, offloading the problem to the creator. If you feel indie, that's enough.

As these shifting IGF criteria show, indie games have been mostly recognizable through negative definitions, in terms of what they're not. The 'other' against which indie games have defined themselves has been the big-budget, big-studio, mainstream 'AAA' game. Working from Bruce Shelley's 2001 'Guidelines for Developing Successful Games,' Juul argues that the simplest way to elaborate the indie ethos is by inverting the recipe for a mainstream hit. Mainstream games seek broad audiences, strive for easy-to-use interfaces, and value glossy production values; indie games are targeted at niche audiences, are deliberately vague and mystifying, and employ visual styles that signal their low budgets. Mainstream games seek massive, epic scope and aim to launch franchises; indie games are unheroic, anti-epic, small, and one-offs. Mainstream games exist to entertain their players; indie games scoff at 'fun.'

Juul manages to come up with only two positive definitions of indie games. The first is that they seek 'authenticity.' But since this is such a vague term, it leads him back to the negative definition. How do they demonstrate their authenticity? By differentiating themselves from mainstream games – which stand for 'inauthenticity' – in the manner just described, or by proclaiming their financial, aesthetic, or cultural independence … from mainstream games. The second definition is that indie games are 'personal.' Juul sees this emphasis on the personal as the main definitional strategy of the 2012 documentary *Indie Game: The Movie*, which he says did more than anything else to popularize and concretize the genre. Focusing on individuals and small teams, the film 'cast independent game development in the familiar story of a struggling artist, working on a deeply personal project and finally making it to public recognition.' Yet Juul finds this definition of indie-ness to be as disappointing as the other ones, not only because it is once again a negative definition – the personal nature of indie development is an inversion of the impersonal, team-based, corporate model of mainstream games – but also because it is such a familiar, hackneyed way of looking at artistic creation. Just as auteur theory in cinema allowed team-based film production to fit into more familiar individual-centric narratives borrowed from literature, music, and visual art, *Indie Game*'s stress on the personal could be seen as just another sellout: a way to make 'video games palatable as cultural works by showing creation stories similar to well-known creation stories from other forms.' (It probably goes without saying – as someone writing a deeply personal book about a deeply personal videogame project – that the strategy totally worked for me.)

Juul's resistance to seeing videogame production through the more familiar cultural lens of other art forms is understandable given his academic trajectory. He started his career as a game theorist working to express what was unique about games – what made them different from novels or films, why it didn't make sense to just impose models from other disciplines, why game studies was needed in the first place. So it's no surprise that he mentions but doesn't stress the connections of indie games to other DIY forms. Early in *Handmade Pixels*, he writes,

> independent games are inspired by and have been compared to various other 'independent' forms, such as cinema and punk music, in their rejection of a compromised status quo and in the assumed democratization of video games through DIY tools. But independent *games* appeared at a different historical time than did other types of independence, and the ideas they incorporated were different than those incorporated in independent music or cinema.

With that, he drops the subject. In one sense, I can see his point. My desire to see indie games as a reiteration of modernism and punk is just as personal as his desire to see them as separate: just as it makes sense for a game scholar to want to see games as distinctive, it makes sense for a scholar of modernism and fan of punk to see all his interests coalesce. My experience in the classroom in San Diego – my students' refusal to engage with *Gone Home* – had stayed with me as a warning of the dangers of conflating my teenage enthusiasms with my students', my sad middle-aged need to force a connection with the next generation.

But even Juul can't entirely ignore the correspondences. For one thing, indie games and their antecedents clearly came into being in similar ways. At one point, Juul notes that indie games must be understood in the context of the rising popularity of videogames in general. As more and more people start playing games, it becomes possible for creators to target small niches within the videogame-playing public. This is exactly how modernist literature came about. Universal education began to increase rates of literacy in many countries throughout the nineteenth century so that, by the start of the twentieth century, Virginia Woolf declared in 'A Letter to a Young Poet,' 'For the first time in history there are readers – a large body of people, occupied in business, in sport, in nursing their grandfathers, in tying up parcels behind counters – they all read now.' What had been a monolithic reading public, conceived as a whole, began to fragment – so that there were books for kids, books for working people, books for people who desperately wanted you to know that they were not working people. Noting the connection to modernist avant-gardes, Juul accepts that 'some independent and art games can be seen as a similar response to the broadening of the video game audience, a way for self-identified game connoisseurs to demon-strate a particularly refined taste, now that most people play video games.' This leads him to recognize 'a central contradiction in independent games, that they can both democratize video games by enabling more diverse and DIY development *and* rarify game consumption by catering to the tastes of a selected few.' It's the story of the Hogarth Press all over again: on the one hand, demo-cratically DIY, allowing anyone to say whatever they want in their own way; on the other, for the most part reaching a limited, privi-leged, elite audience.

Woolf's Hogarth Press also gives precedent for debates in indie games around the figure of the 'bohemian entrepreneur' – 'ideal-ized types who, by running a company, can keep their own hours, stay out and sleep in late, and spend a significant part of the work-day in coffee shops.' Juul uses the bohemian entrepreneur to drive a wedge between indie games and punk. As *Indie Game: The Movie* clearly shows, the allure of indie games is the promise of doing what you want, refusing to compromise, expressing yourself … and also getting rich. Both of the games profiled, *Fez* and *Super Meat Boy*, were huge commercial hits. One of the main interview subjects, Jonathan Blow, filmed in his hilltop San Francisco home, famously bought a $150,000 Tesla when *Braid* blew up. (A 2012 *Atlantic* profile of Blow begins, 'Like many wealthy people, Jonathan Blow vividly remembers the moment he became rich.') As Juul points out, doctrinaire DIY-ethic punk culture would never stand for this: '*punk rock was* [sic] *most definitely not about being an entrepreneur*, however independently.' Yet this contradiction has been part of the DIY arts from the beginning. Johnny Rotten got rich. Carrie Brownstein did a commercial for American Express. Hogarth was a successful business; despite publishing badass books like *Three Guineas*, it made the Woolfs a good income.

The debates around riot grrrl have also been replayed in indie games. Just as riot grrrl can be read as failing to live up to its own ideals of inclusion, so too have indie games been called out on the incompleteness of their revolution. If indie games were exciting because, suddenly, anyone could make them, all voices could be heard, any kind of narrative could be told – why was it, for example, that every creator profiled in *Indie Game: The Movie* was a white, middle-class man?

The same year that *Indie Game: The Movie* was released, a book was published that exposed the narrowness of its vision: Anna Anthropy's amply subtitled *Rise of the Videogame Zinesters: How Freaks, Normals, Amateurs, Artists, Dreamers, Drop-Outs, Queers, Housewives, and People Like You Are Taking Back an Art Form.* Anthropy's argument begins from a representational void. 'As a queer transgendered woman in 2012,' she writes, 'I have to strain to find any game that's about a queer woman, to find any game that resembles my own experience. Mostly, videogames are about men shooting men in the face.' Why is this the case? In what is perhaps the most compact and compelling account of the relationship between the material realities of videogame production and their artistic failings, she argues that 'the problem with videogames is that they're created by a small, insular group of people' – that 'digital games largely come from within a single culture.' Because they require advanced technical skills to produce, because those skills have generally been taught to white men at colleges with expensive tuition, because those people demand and are granted high salaries, because a lot of them are needed to make a single game, because it would be foolish for big studios to risk throwing their money away on any title that wasn't likely to recoup their massive investment in it – for all these reasons,

Anthropy argues, 'videogames as they're commonly conceived today both come from and contain exactly one perspective.' 'It should be terrifying,' she continues, 'that an entire art form can be dominated by a single perspective, that a small and privileged group has a monopoly on the creation of art.'

Anthropy's book is hopeful, even utopian – just not about indie games as they are depicted in *Indie Game: The Movie*. The kinds of 'rich white dudes' featured in that documentary 'were professional programmers before they came to videogames.' She's bored by creators who already worked in the industry, already had the cultural and financial capital to make it, but then became frustrated by the lack of expressive possibility in commercial videogame production. She's bored by game engines like Unity that make it possible for small, technically skilled teams to make games that are indistinguishable from commercial blockbusters. Instead, she's excited about tools that make it possible for *anyone* to make a videogame, just as photocopiers made it possible for *anyone* to publish a book. Indeed, for Anthropy the connection to the zine culture of punk and riot grrrl is so important that she puts it in the title of her book. In the most utopian passage in *Rise of the Videogame Zinesters*, she writes,

> I like the idea of games as zines: as transmissions of ideas and culture from person to person, as personal artifacts instead of impersonal creations by teams of forty-five artists and fifteen programmers, in the case of *Gears of War 2*. The Internet in particular has made self-publishing and distributing games both possible and easy. Authors are able not only to put their works online, but to find audiences for them. Publishers want to be gatekeepers to the creation of videogames, but the Internet has opened those gates. Currently, the only real barrier to game creation is the technical ability to design and create games – and that, too, is a problem that is in the process of being solved.

The problem is being solved, she argues, by tools like GameMaker and, especially, the incredibly user-friendly web-based platform Twine: game-making tools that non-experts can learn in a few hours. 'What I want from videogames,' Anthropy says at one point, 'is a plurality of voices.' Accessible technologies like Twine, which cost nothing, are easy to learn, and whose games can be published for free online, are the way to this goal.

Gamergate put this utopian narrative to the test. The less that is said about the specific origins of the #GamerGate hashtag, I feel, the better. A boyfriend felt wronged; a conspiracy theory was hatched. But it is important that at the centre of the controversy was a game made in Twine: Zoe Quinn's *Depression Quest*.

Coming at it from the perspective of a literature scholar and music nerd, it can be baffling how *Depression Quest* could have inspired all the controversy it did. It presents something utterly familiar in both media: a deeply personal story about dealing with depression, trying to live through it, trying to make yourself understood by those around you, trying to make the least-bad decisions in a tough situation. It does add a brilliant twist, doing something that couldn't be done in any other medium. The game unfolds mostly like a novel, with some images and some music but mostly long passages of text. Each of these passages ends with a series of choices: will you go out or stay in, adopt a kitten, go into therapy, go off your meds? The ingenious thing is that only a few choices can actually be clicked on, and how many are clickable depends on how depressed you are. The game is thus a depression simulator: it aims to show people who don't suffer from depression what depression is like. You can see the right choice, you know what it is, but you just can't do it. And the worse you feel, the more limited your choices are.

There were many targets in Gamergate – anyone not a straight, white, teenage, middle-class boy, basically – and the nastiness took many forms. But Zoe Quinn was arguably the main target, and much of the nastiness centred on *Depression Quest*. In 2014, when Valve made the game available through the indie-focused 'Greenlight' program on its Steam store – the same PC-based distribution platform that challenged the dominance of consoles and physical media sold in stores and thus played a crucial role in the rise of indie games – all hell broke loose. Quinn was doxxed, she received rape threats in the mail and death threats over the phone. A coordinated campaign was launched to flood the game's Steam and Metacritic pages with angry, paranoid reviews.

Many attempts have been made to understand why Gamergate happened at all, and why it happened in response to *Depression Quest*. The most convincing argument I've read is in 'Your Humanity Is in Another Castle,' an article by Katherine Cross and Anita Sarkeesian, herself a target of Gamergate backlash (her crime: arguing that female characters should be present in video-games as something other than projections of male fantasies). In a brilliant turn, Cross and Sarkeesian argue that Gamergate itself unfolded according to a game logic, in which male gamers cast themselves as 'valiant defenders of cyberspace' and 'women as henpecking invaders who will take the boys' toys.' These male gamers then teamed up, using all the skills they'd learned through endless hours of playing multi-player games, to rove in mobs and coordinate their attacks, to take down their enemies. These gamers were motivated by what Cross and Sarkeesian call a 'terror dream.' Gaming is their safe space: bullied at school or at work, it is where they can band together to act out their fantasies, do all the things they can't in waking life. The fear that motivated Gamergate was that 'someone somewhere is going to take gaming away from the nerdy fans who've huddled around its warmth as a refuge from the world's bullying.' They responded to this existential threat with maximum violence.

To me, the amazing thing is not that these gamers felt threatened by *Depression Quest* or Sarkeesian's critique, but that they noticed them at all. Juul argues, and I agree, that the indie-game movement comes out of the fragmentation of the videogame-playing audience – from the fact that when there are enough people playing games, even niche tastes can be served. Gamergate shows how incomplete the fragmentation of the videogame market is today – that it's still underway, the ice floe still cracking. The average fan of superhero movies won't get outraged by challenging art films about depression, for a simple reason: the fragmentation of the filmgoing audience has advanced to the point that they will never hear about, much less see, those films. In the world of books, music, and movies, mechanisms are in place to make sure that no one needs to encounter anything that doesn't fit their tastes. On the one hand, this is a comfortable situation, protecting avant-garde artists from the avalanche of hate that descended on Zoe Quinn. On the other, it's lonely: what you gain in safety you lose in the ability to reach an audience, change minds – and make a living.

In her 2014 *New York Times Magazine* piece 'Twine, The Video-Game Technology for All,' Laura Hudson tells the story of Gamergate and outlines the role that Twine games like *Depression Quest* played in it. She focuses not on Quinn, though, but on a fascinating developer named Porpentine Charity Heartscape (Porpentine for short), known for the dark, claustrophobic, sickly-sweet worlds she creates. Much of the article focuses on Hudson's conversations with Porpentine about the realities of making ends meet as a creator of avant-garde videogames. Porpentine has rent to pay and, having begun hormone therapy two years prior, medical bills to pay. At one point Hudson asks Porpentine whether she would want her games to appear on Steam, the platform 'where *Depression Quest* found a significant audience but also significant harassment.' Porpentine replies that, yes, she's certainly interested. 'It's a tension that comes up often when I talk to female Twine developers,' Hudson writes: 'the push and pull between going big and staying small, between art and commerce, between the comparative safety (and poverty) of smaller spaces and the main-stream visibility that allowed Zoe Quinn's game to reach so many people, even as it made her a target.'

After reading Hudson's piece, I became obsessed with Porpentine's games, especially *With Those We Love Alive*, a lush, overripe

masterpiece of dystopian sci-fi. You play as an artist in an impossible situation. Recognized as an incomparable sculptor in steel
and bone, you've been summoned to the capital, where the evil
Empress's body, slowly decaying, needs mending. You loathe her,
but your task is literally to build her body, to keep her alive. Your
genuine loathing for the Empress turns over easily into rampant,
self-destructive desire. At one point, the Empress passes by, leaving
in her wake 'smears of ichor like the stain of rotten fruit' – which
'putrid nectar' you promptly 'lick [...] from the ground until the
ground is clean,' leaving your breath smelling 'like you've been
eating the refuse of an orchard or a toilet.'

In 2017, I put a grant together to bring Porpentine to San Diego
State. There was a new, generous fund in place at SDSU to bring
high-profile speakers to campus, and as Porpentine had just been
selected for that year's Whitney Biennial, she fit the bill. The
experience turned out to be one of the more awkward ones of
my life. We had lunch, we walked around campus, Porpentine
gave a Twine workshop, there was a big interview with a camera
crew there to film it. But all day, it was clear that Porpentine didn't
want to be there: she wasn't rude or difficult, she just seemed
uncomfortable, out of her element. Preparing for the interview,
I'd come up with what I thought was a really great question. 'Did
you feel like the protagonist of *With Those We Love Alive* at the
Whitney Biennial – selected by some ravenous beast of a cultural
institution, summoned to the capital of the art establishment,
forced into an impossible double bind, revolted by and flattered
by orthodox recognition?' As the day proceeded, I realized that I
was the Whitney Biennial of my question, I was the Empress. I
was a representative of orthodoxy, of the establishment, of a
cultural institution. She wasn't there because she wanted to be,
because she recognized me as a peer, because she wanted to
spread the gospel about Twine. She was there because the indie-
game model of the bourgeois entrepreneur didn't work for artists
like her. She had rent and medical bills to pay.

As with most things related to videogames, I first heard about Gamergate from Craig. In the years I've been working on this book, in addition to visiting Craig's house in the woods, I've kept in regular touch with him via Skype. At first, when it seemed like the game might come out at any minute, I'd Skype with Craig every couple of months. When it became clear it would be a while, we talked about once a year, usually in the summer. However infrequent, these chats would be epically long – minimum two and a half hours, maximum of five. Craig would catch me up on what he had been up to, I would get the odd question in, I'd take notes. Often I'd feel like Craig was drifting off-topic, focusing on the wrong things, not talking enough about 'expression' or 'authenticity' or his hatred of AAA games, but my journalistic skills weren't sufficiently advanced to allow me to interject myself with force, to direct the flow of conversation. But then, reading back through my notes months or years later, I'd see that Craig was talking about exactly the most relevant stuff, exactly the questions I would have asked if I'd been able to go back in time, that keeping my mouth shut was the right move.

I Skyped with Craig in August 2014, the month that the #GamerGate hashtag first began to circulate. It was early morning and I had a coffee somewhere offscreen. Craig's daughter had been born the month before and Craig seemed suitably transformed. 'From the day before the birth,' he told me, 'it seemed like we entered into a dreamworld that we have not really exited.' He went to get his daughter and brought her on camera, but his internet connection got shaky. 'I'm seeing cute blobs!' I said.

The elation faded twenty minutes into our conversation, when we started talking about social media. I was telling him how afraid I was of it, how I only used it to make myself visible to help me get a job, how I had in fact initially signed up for Twitter just so I could get in touch with him to invite him to speak to my class, and how I would stop using it as soon as I got a job (as indeed I did). He said he'd been checking Twitter incessantly of late.

Ukraine, Gaza, Ferguson: it had been a rough couple of weeks. 'The ugliness that has existed is rearing its head.'

That's when he told me about Gamergate, something so new that in my notes I spelled it with a space and no capitals, 'gamer gate':

> In videogame culture, there's this *horrible* saga going on in the last few weeks, in amongst all this other horribleness. It feels like there's going to be a before and an after. All the sort of simmering ugliness that has existed for a long time has now asserted itself with such force, and has made such a mess. It feels like this culture, whatever it is, had its various different components to it, but now there's a kind of binary opposition – there's a divide, between *two* camps, and it probably seems like it will remain pretty fraught. This situation won't just dissipate.

I asked what the polarization was.

> There is a crowd of people who have identified themselves so strongly with a particular type of videogame culture that they feel is under threat, because there's a more progressive element that has been pushing the conversation forward in the last few years. There's a defensiveness that has turned into an aggressive attitude, and that aggressive attitude has run completely amok.

I asked if there were any real arguments on that side.

> They will pride themselves on being eminently rational, but in fact their whole reason is emotional, and the rationality is coming from little scraps of things that appear rational. [...] Anyways [*deep sigh*] it's very distressing. I hope there's a way forward. But the image that I have is that videogame culture has become this smoking crater

in the ground, and that we would be best served just walking away and starting afresh.

I asked if he was really ready to abandon videogames altogether.

Even with *Sworcery*, even to communicate with somebody, you've got to put it in the category of a videogame. But the way it was created and initially presented, I even avoided that label. You can't get very far with that, but I think philosophically there's a reason to stake out a new medium involving, you know, narrative and interactivity and computing that doesn't have the history, culture, expectations and baggage.

I then said how useless 'videogames' could feel as a label.

Yeah, it's descriptive of videogames. But it's not descriptive of a whole bunch of things that are not quite videogames. With *Sworcery* I didn't want to think of it that way. I wanted to think about, hypothetically, if there was a culture that grew up differently – if technology intersected culture differently. […] Even with *Sworcery* as a point-and-click adventure, which is a traditional genre of videogames, we weren't trying to replicate that: we were trying to create something built from scratch, with some of the love that we remember from having played these kinds of things, not just take techniques and methods off the shelf. […] Which, at the time, wasn't that much of a leap, because the iPhone was so new and the iPad was so new. Expectations hadn't been built up. It really did feel like a blank canvas. Certainly as blank a canvas as we've had in our generation.

I said this all sounded a lot like modernism's sense of completely starting over, of 'culture year zero,' of 'make it new.' Then I asked if it felt like the next project was moving back into conventional videogames rather than away from them.

> Well, yeah, a little bit. Because we're building it around a controller and because it will go to one of the big notable services like Steam or PlayStation … We might build it as something fresh and new, and I think we're keeping that sensibility in mind. But the audience we're going to need to connect with is an audience that's built up around videogames. We're going to need to bridge that gap.

I asked if this watershed moment, this line drawn in the sand, this before-and-after, paradigm-shifting moment (Craig was right, it was), this 'gamer gate' would affect the way he personally thought about videogames.

> Nope [*very definitive*]. Not really … [*less definitive*].
> My feeling about what we're building – we've done so much concocting and done so much exploration, that the phase we're in now is, you know, we're putting in the hours to push it towards the goalposts that we set up a little while back. The decisions we're making are smaller. They're not big and broad and conceptual. There are still story/character type decisions to be made … But I don't think this will affect that.

JETT was on its path – but that path already took 'into account some of the conversation that's going on':

> Just meaning that … with *Sworcery* there's an equal number of male and female characters. That's something that didn't take any particular effort, but I just had to notice, and Jori pointed it out: that hey, like, why not just keep an eye out and see if you can do it, and it didn't prove that difficult, it just involved changing the gender of the wolf!

I'm trying to just stick with the values and principles I have. Part of that is creating a videogame that isn't reliant on aggression and violence and that in fact allows people to exercise more benign thought processes and aspects of their character. And the other is to present a world that isn't the sort of typical gender split, or doesn't approach things in that way. That's been in the DNA of the project from the moment it came into existence. So there's no big change I need to consider there. […] In fact, I have looked at this ongoing conversation and this drama and then looked back at the project and asked of it, 'Is there something I need to consider?' and then my feeling is that we made the right bets a little while back and I'm happy with creating this, I think this is what I want to create.

I asked if he felt compelled to take any action in the midst of all this ugliness – to get involved, especially on Twitter, where it was all playing out, where he had a considerable audience, which was so connected to the success of *Sworcery*, but on which he had been silent in the years since.

Because I'm a step away from everything these days, I don't feel like I need to be taking any particular action now, but I just think about what it'll look like next year or the year after when it is time to bring the project to an audience that is … mired in drama.

After that we dropped the thread, moved on to other things.

In our future summer Skypes, there would always be the moment where I would ask some variation of my 'So: indie games' question. Generally, Craig would be much more interested in talking about some detail of development than climbing onto a pulpit to discuss the fate of an entire movement or artistic medium. But sometimes he'd bite.

This was the case in June 2017, when we kept going back to the question of whether the moment for indie games was over – whether, by the time the next game came out, that term would even have any meaning. The sorts of games that were doing really well in 2006–2012, he told me, were not doing well now. *N+*, *Braid*, *Journey*, *Fez*, they defined an era – the time Jesper Juul refers to as 'peak indie' and Craig called 'the era of people stroking their beards and talking about stuff.' But *Journey* and *Fez* had also closed the book on that era. They were the culmination of a period of development that, once it reached its goal, ended in 2012. That year represented a shift for Craig personally, the year he moved to the woods, but was also the end of a cycle for videogames. With games jams, with tools like Unity, development became *so* accessible, *so* desirable, that it all exploded. It used to be that if you got your game on Steam, you had a platform, you had an audience, you were set. But by 2017, Steam had started letting *everything* into its store, so that acceptance was no longer a golden ticket. There was way too much out there. Looking back, there was some kind of sweet spot – necessarily brief – when it was easy *enough* so that *some* people could Do It Themselves, could make something new and daring if they worked really hard, but it wasn't so easy that absolutely everyone could. Some friction was actually useful. Without it, there were too many games, too little space for many of them to get noticed, the market was flooded, so people lost interest.

This included the big studios, Microsoft and Sony, who had actively courted indie developers around 2013–14. Craig had always hoped that Sony would be involved with the new game in some way, had indeed been developing it around the PlayStation controller. But it seemed like that was over, too. Sony was no longer funding artsy stuff.

Even Craig had lost interest. He admired some of the stuff that Double Fine was doing, he admired Annapurna's recent game *What Remains of Edith Finch*, a *Gone-Home*–esque piece in which you wander around in a house in the Pacific Northwest in order to reconstruct a narrative. But that didn't mean he was interested in actually playing these kinds of games. 'Even though I'm in the artsy, boutiquey space, I don't have much patience with that,' he said. If he was being honest with himself, he would rather shoot a robot dinosaur. This was the first time I heard a word that would feature prominently in Juul's account of the period from 2015 to the present: this was the era of the 'indiepocalypse.'

The topic of Gamergate came up again when we talked during the summer of 2018. With four years to reflect on it, Craig's feelings had developed.

It had been a year since we'd spoken, and in many ways the conversation was difficult to distinguish from the previous one. Work was still going slowly. After two hours of progress reports, we turned to the more general question of the relationship between videogames and politics. This was one of those moments for me to insert myself, to ask a meaningful question, to ask him whether he still believed in his old vision of making a game, building a platform for himself, and then using that platform to deliver a powerful message about climate change. It was an idealistic vision that excited me when he first told me about it on our walk up the Summit in 2013 – the sort of idealistic vision that drew me to modernism, punk, riot grrrl, and indie games in the first place. I wondered whether it now seemed childish to him, or if the sense of urgency was still there.

Prompted by my question, he spoke, slowly and carefully, masterfully and articulately, for ten minutes straight. I knew better than to interrupt. His tone was reflective, somewhat bleak, self-recriminating but self-forgiving, an honest dialogue of the self with the self. He started with his decision to stop studying climate science. 'When I bailed on climate science,' he said, 'I chose a life with adventures and enjoyable, productive work and I had an idea about how to sort of justify that to myself … like *sort of*.' The 'build a platform' plan always seemed a little hollow, even to him. It came out of hopelessness – a sense that pursuing the problem directly, taking the climate-science route, wouldn't actually achieve anything and wouldn't work for his personality. He didn't see himself in the role of 'shrill activist' – he wouldn't be able to sustain it. He would have gone off the rails after ten years of being disappointed and beaten down. And, realistically, how would he get a job with all this, have a family? Okay, he told himself, the problem is one of communication, the big gap is a cultural problem. So he would gain some skills and push things from that side. He could do that. He'd be a bit like Studio Ghibli in post-war Japan. 'They wanted to tell stories that would go out to the next generation. You make *My Neighbor Totoro* and you develop a feeling of what Japanese culture could be. And I don't know what the measurable effect of that was, but it was something.'

For a moment I could hear Craig working up his old enthusiasm for the plan – but just as quickly, the air was let out. 'So, you know … *yeah*' – deeply ironic – 'in a hopeless situation that's the cushy route that you could take.' Of his decision to abandon his studies in climate science, he said, 'I think it was a retreat that was justifiable at the time, reasonable at the time, maybe still reasonable in retrospect. But I think it was a retreat to some degree.' This led to his thoughts on Gamergate:

> Similarly, moving out here, there were a bunch of reasons that this was the path that I was always hopeful for, and then circumstances made it possible, and I'm glad for it. This is where I would want to have been whatever the case. But it is still another retreat, I guess. And I associate that a bit with just not doing one's duty.
>
> And another one was, I just went offline in 2012. My duties were complete, I would not have an online presence, I got back to work. And then, you know, the Gamergate warzone passed through the industry and steamrolled a lot of people. And I wasn't online, I was aware of it, and I could see people I knew getting steamrolled, and seeing just how bent out of shape everything was getting, but I

didn't know what to do. I mean, you could definitely go out and say, 'Okay, I'm back, steamroll me!' or whatever. But then you get into this thing where you need to be strategic because you've got a kid or two kids and you've got a home life and a family and that has to be a big priority in your life, especially if you're not a superhero, and you've got to get your sleep and you've got to put in the work. So then how much energy or bandwidth do you have on top of that to invest anywhere? But then that's not a good line because … you're maybe not as selfish as you *could* be, because you are thinking of your family and your community, but that's still a form of selfishness, where I'm not trying to work on the broader community nor am I trying to solve the world's problems, which is kind of an absurd path, so … I don't know.

Sworcery has paid my paycheque up until now. But my first duty is to get this project done in a good enough way that I can continue to have an income and a job, to continue to have a family and a house, and also to have enough so that I can continue to live, save a certain amount of money. And it's not like the *Sworcery* thing was like, a bonanza, with cartoon money. It was a certain size that allowed this much platform *if I'm strategic*, and if I put a bunch of things off … and I'm super grateful for it. But that's not like notoriety or money that you can do much with. What would be nice and the way that I imagined it was, you plug away and you try to build something and you're in your forties and hopefully you've accomplished some of that. You've got to build some sort of platform to stand on, so you have bandwidth. And that doesn't happen instantly, so you've got to put in that work. I *could* imagine some version of this where I have the bandwidth and the interest to start to engage in some fashion, but what form that could take, I mean … You know, people say, 'Think global, act local,' and that's also a bit of a retreat these days, but what else can you really do? I remain open and interested but up until now I've just been so deep into trying to execute my duties as project lead and a father and a husband that it's like: that's enough …

And not to exonerate myself completely, if I have an evening off I'm going to play *God of War* or I'm watching TV with Jori. I'm not doing heroic things.

The questions that this chapter has been leading up to are, of course, was *Sworcery* an indie game, and is JETT? And the answers it has been leading up to, of course, are that it's complicated.

Sworcery definitely had aesthetic independence – it looked different from other games in 2011, with its peculiar use of pixels, hard and lush at once. One look at it and you knew a page had been turned. But then styles changed: pixels became a bit of an indie cliché, *Fez* was the last game to make them look fresh, and that was in 2012 – a lifetime ago. By the time Craig was starting to work on JETT, pixels felt played out, and the fresh thing to do aesthetically felt like high-quality, high-res 3D. These are the confusing eddies you find yourself in when your genre identity is defined negatively, when what you are is just the opposite of something else – it means your own identity is never stable, always tied to the Other, mirroring it, so that if it picks up a bit of your reflection you need to become something other than yourself, which circles back to your becoming the thing you initially set out to avoid.

Sworcery clearly had cultural independence. Its goal was to rebalance the mind – about as lofty as you can get – and this wasn't just something my overheated academic brain had cooked up; Craig actually had it in mind. If that aim faded a bit in the process of getting it done and bringing it to market, took a bit of a back seat in the midst of that hectic rush, that didn't mean it was any less genuine. JETT was no different: in rejecting violence and a straightforward narrative of colonial conquest, in its quest to develop mechanics that would make its player approach the unknown with respect and care, in its aim to 'exercise benign thought processes,' it was absolutely in the same spirit. And who knows, maybe the fact that they were wrapping all this up in a more recognizably videogamey package, with 3D graphics and a conventional controller, just meant it would reach a broader audience and make a greater impact. It wasn't proper DIY if it wasn't trying to attain maximum reach, according to my own theory.

But the question of financial independence was fraught. *Sworcery* had been made in a small studio, an 'independent' studio. But Capy still existed to make money, was still a commercial enterprise. And of course, it had made money, immortalized in the '$1 MILLION' frame from *Indie Game: The Movie*. Money had been part of that narrative, the narrative of the white male bohemian entrepreneur who left a job in the industry to do what he wanted, on his own terms – but with the help of a lot of technically skilled collaborators, with lots of financial and cultural capital thrown in, a lot of privilege, and in such a way as to make enough money to buy a house in the woods and tune out the outside world for the next decade.

Were things any simpler for JETT? Well, it was initially entirely self-financed, so in that sense its financial independence was complete. Quibble if you must about how Craig acquired his war chest, but he had it, and he used it to make exactly the kind of game he wanted in exactly the way he wanted to make it. The long-term goal was to sell the game, to support his family, to earn a living. But he could have done that by following the many conventional opportunities that were open to him, which would have been more lucrative and a whole lot easier. He and Patrick chose to make JETT because they had a vision of what they wanted to make, refused to compromise, and saw that making the game themselves was the only way to do it. That was the DIY ethic: a principled, intentional belief in the artistic and political necessity of working outside conventional, commercial modes of production. Unity was his duplicator.

That was the situation, at least, until the summer of 2019, when Superbrothers signed a multi-million-dollar deal with Sony.

PART III

THE END OF THE RAINBOW

7.

The day I started to write this book, there was a massive storm. I was in my office at San Diego State, my notes and outlines spread out in front of me. The rain was falling so hard that I couldn't see more than a few feet out my window. But just as I started to write, the rain suddenly stopped, and the brightest, widest rainbow I'd ever seen appeared, intense and vivid against the black background of the storm clouds. I immediately took it as an omen.

At that point in time, 2015, the world knew only one thing about Superbrothers' next game. If you went to www.superbrothershq.com and clicked on 'videogames,' you would have seen a brief, unspecific entry for an 'unannounced new project (in progress)' that was minimally described as 'the second videogame from superbrothers, in the works for ages but still a few years off,' 'a follow-up of sorts to *sworcery* only with no sword, no sworcery and no hard-edged pixels.' Though it was barely described, the videogame did have a logo. It sat above the description: a pair of headphones whose earcups were connected by a big, bright, shining rainbow.

It was like magic. The moment I started writing about that videogame, its logo appeared, projected in the sky.

Whenever I was feeling particularly gloomy about the prospect of the game or my book ever seeing the light of day, I would think of that rainbow. Despite the mounting evidence that this project might be doomed, for them and for me, I couldn't shake the feeling that it was in fact charmed, that everything was always just about to fall into place. This intuition of cosmic alignment was validated five years later, on June 11, 2020, at 4:36 p.m. The game – now known to the world as *JETT: The Far Shore* – had, at long last, been officially announced to the world. The fact that the game had been announced at all was cause for celebration. Yet the way it happened was just ridiculous. It came in the splashiest manner imaginable, as part of the official reveal for Sony's next-generation PS5 console, an event watched by ten million people around the globe and covered everywhere in the press. Sony had made the decision to focus their reveal event on games rather than hardware. In the wooden words that opened the event, Sony Interactive Entertainment CEO Jim Ryan explained that the idea was to showcase how the PS5 had 'inspired developers to create new experiences that are transformative in how they look, sound, and feel.'

There followed an hour of clips for blockbusters like GTA V, *Fortnite*, and *Spider Man: Miles Morales*. Sandwiched somewhere in the middle were two minutes of steppes, socialist-realist architecture, and space cathedrals. It was JETT: *The Far Shore*, 'coming for Holiday 2020,' and the whole world now knew it.

The announcement of this book was a little less splashy. It had happened the same year as the rainbow, in 2015, when JETT was still called *The Future* and the Sony deal was far beyond the horizon.

Early that year, a series of chats with Craig led me to believe that the release of the game, whatever its name, was just around the corner, and that I needed to hurry up and start writing. Since books are generally announced a year before they appear, the first step was getting a cover and a description together for the publisher's catalogue. A series of rushed emails ensued with my editor, Alana. We wanted an image from the game for the cover, but Craig was too busy finishing it up to give us one. So in the end we decided to run a blank rectangle with the following text running diagonally across it, which we hoped would come across as both tantalizing and mysterious: 'Cover image embargoed until game release in 2016.' Thus did my book become known to the world.

It turned out that 2015 was a big year for the game and for my book. I finally got to meet Craig's partners on the project, the programmer Patrick McAllister, a.k.a. Pine Scented and the musician C. Andrew Rohrmann, a.k.a Andy, a.k.a. scntfc (there were a lot of aliases to manage that year). I spent a week shadowing them as they worked on a crucial aspect of the game, Ground Control. I finally got my first playable build. I even travelled to Japan to meet Patrick.

It is also the year that I first heard the term 'development hell.'

Development hell is the great cliché in narratives of videogame development, the gaming community's version of writer's block. Legends abound of games that take decades to produce, with huge, overcomplicated narratives that can't be fit into a playable frame, insanely ambitious graphics and gameplay that can't be achieved with the available hardware (a moving target anyway, since platforms are always changing), huge egos that can't be made to work together, and overweening studios constantly demanding stupid rewrites. The classic example is *Duke Nukem Forever*, which took more or less that long (the fifteen years from 1996–2011) to produce.

The narrative is especially prevalent in the indie-game world. The classic example here is Phil Fish's *Fez*, whose development hell is so memorably captured in *Indie Game: The Movie*. Announced in 2007, *Fez* won a visual design award in 2008 at the Independent Games Festival while it was still in early development. (Fish accepted the award dressed in a red fez.) This award in turn won the game a rabid online fanbase that clamoured for a quick release. Fish parlayed the award into a sizeable loan from the always-benevolent Canadian government, which allowed him to quit his day job, start his own hyperbolically named studio (Polytron Corporation), and begin full-scale development in earnest. In 2009, Fish announced that *Fez* would come out in 2010. In 2010, he announced that it would be delayed until 2011. That was the year he told the directors of *Indie Game* that he would kill himself if he didn't release his game. It finally came out in 2012, by which time he had been so demoralized by the hype and pressure of development hell that he publicly announced he was quitting videogames.

JETT: *The Far Shore* wasn't anywhere near that breaking point at the start of 2015. Craig and Patrick had only been actively developing the game for a little over two years. Patrick was the technical half of the duo responsible for the game. Craig was the artist/designer/deep-thinker. Patrick was the programmer, the nuts-and-bolts guy, the one responsible for making sure that the laws of physics applied in the gameworld, that when you drove your ship into a wall, it blew up.

Craig and Patrick had met in Toronto in 2007 when they both worked at Koei Canada. Patrick is American, from Oklahoma, but had studied Computer Science and Philosophy at the University of Waterloo in Ontario. This peculiar combination of subjects informed his somewhat jaundiced view of the videogame industry: he liked playing them, he was good at making them, but he struggled with the question of whether they mattered. Craig was asking similar questions, so they got along and decided they would like to work on an indie project together if the opportunity ever arose. But Patrick had been offered a job at Koei's headquarters in Japan, left Canada, met his future wife, and decided to stay. He had followed the story of *Sworcery* with interest and, seeing how successful it had been, decided to leave his stable job at Koei and join the indie ranks when Craig floated the idea of working together on the next game. Married by this point and with a kid on the way, Patrick had stayed in Japan, which meant that he and Craig, situated on opposite ends of the planet, worked on a twelve-hour time-shift. Their production schedule was perfectly mirrored. When Craig was working, Patrick was sleeping. While Patrick slept, Craig worked. The sun never set on the Superbrothers/Pine Scented videogame empire.

They still had plenty of reason to be sunny. Patrick had only quit his job at Koei in the spring of 2013. And there was no outside pressure, because they hadn't announced they were working on a game. The very small set of people who knew about it, myself included, were bound to secrecy by non-disclosure agreements. There were no rabid fans pestering them on Twitter about release dates, no sinister obsessives trying to hack their accounts for screenshots or demos. There were no studio executives breathing down their necks about deadlines or distributors threatening to bail. A huge advantage of working independently, self-funded with savings (Patrick) or the self-replenishing treasure chest of *Sworcery* cash (Craig: the game continued to sell well) was that they weren't accountable to anyone else's release schedule or hype cycle. As Craig explained to me countless times over the years, this was perhaps the most appealing thing to him about the 'indie' model, and he was acting very deliberately, having experienced all the manic pressure that followed *Sworcery*'s announcement and having witnessed all the chaos that swirled around Phil Fish, who was a friend.

But I sometimes wondered if a little bit of outside pressure wouldn't have been helpful. In the two years since I caught my first glimpse of the new game during my visit to the woods of Quebec in 2013, there didn't seem to have been much progress. When I took my first turn behind the controls, it was a flying game where a funny-looking pixellated ship called a 'helijet' flew around in a colourful, mostly empty landscape lightly filled with abstract shapes. There were two modes: the flying mode, where you could rotate the camera around the ship to see it from any angle, and the on-foot mode, where the characters slid around like pieces on a chessboard, without taking steps or swinging their arms.

I had checked in with Craig countless times over the next two years. Though he was always vague about scheduling details, I got the sense that they were planning on releasing around 2015. Not wanting to miss anything, every few weeks I would write emails asking how things were going, or schedule Skype calls where Craig would share his screen and show me what they'd been up to. I always expected it to be radically different from that first glimpse I'd had in the fall of 2013, at which point Patrick had only been full-time for a few months. I'd occasionally have nightmares that the game would be finished in my absence, that I'd miss a crucial phase of development, that details essential for this book would slip through my fingers, never to be recovered.

But every time I saw it, it looked pretty much the same. The ship got a little less pixellated, the landscape a little less colourful, the abstract shapes turned into trees. Instead of sliding around, the characters took steps. There were occasionally things to do. If anything, the game was becoming a little less charming as it lost its roughness – looking more like any other game rather than some strange, handcrafted experiment. But even these changes were almost imperceptibly subtle. Blandness was starting to look like a minor concern. More pressing was the matter of whether it would ever get finished.

In April 2015, Craig invited me to 'shadow' the team for a few weeks. This meant listening in on their daily Skype meetings, where they handed off from one side of the globe to the other – one of them summing up a day of work and the other getting ready to dig in. Given how foggy I was on what they'd been doing and what a day of work on a videogame actually looked like, I was eager to check it out.

At this point in development, Craig and Patrick were working in two-week 'batches,' each focused on some particular task. In the two-week period of my shadowing, they were working on 'Ground Control,' the base/headquarters location in their game world, the place where pilots go to sleep, recharge, and receive their mission instructions. Four mornings in that span, I woke up at 6:30 a.m. Eastern Standard Time (7:30 p.m. Japan Standard Time), ate some breakfast, made the upper half of my body look presentable, and logged on to Skype. I'd say hello and chat with them for a bit. As quickly as possible I'd turn off my video and lurk in the background, watching and listening to their discussion while remaining unseen and unheard.

To do this every day – to speak for an hour or two daily for years on end – you need to like one another. Craig and Patrick clearly did. They would begin with chit-chat, usually about family life. Craig spoke more and more grandly, looking straight into the camera with his pale intense monk's eyes, leaning forward, making broad sweeping gestures with his arms. Patrick spoke less, shifting positions frequently, bringing his leg up onto his chair and back down, slouching so deeply into his seat that his face would sometimes be in danger of sinking right out of the frame.

They talked about the movies they'd seen or games they'd been playing. The main topic in those two weeks was Christopher Nolan's *Interstellar*, which had just come out on DVD. (Neither Patrick nor Craig, having small children, had been to see it in theatres.) The movie had a lot of overlaps with the new game: it was a sci-fi space epic about colonizing a distant planet to ensure a future for a humanity threatened with ecological disaster. Craig considered *Interstellar* a gorgeous catastrophe whose shortcomings could be instructive for them. He liked the basic premise. If the notion of a crop blight in a future where people only ate corn was perhaps 'naïve bioscience,' at least it set a tone: it announced that this was 'a film intended for thinking people, for adults living in the twenty-first century, for people who might have a family and who are thinking about what the future may hold.'

What it lacked, he said, was 'grounding.' On the one hand, it professed respect for science, empiricism, observation, clear-headedness. The hero, played by Matthew McConaughey, is the spokesman for these things, railing against a 'post-truth' future that denies history and dismisses the Apollo landings as propaganda. On the other hand, as soon as the story sets off for space, it becomes a Saturday morning cartoon. McConaughey – dead set against imprecise retellings of cosmic adventures – becomes the protagonist of an imprecise cosmic adventure. Central threads about planetary survival are left murky or barely resolved. The robots are implausible. It ends in utter nonsense. 'I'll go into space with just about any film,' Craig said. 'All I ask for is an internally consistent cosmos.'

After the chit-chat, Craig and Patrick would get down to work, which inevitably unfolded as a furious tug-of-war between the grand and the mundane, brilliant ideas and unbelievably boring details. To convey the idea of respecting and attending to the ecosystem of an alien planet, they needed the ecosystem to respond dynamically to player actions. Birds needed to scatter, or not, depending on how quickly you approached them. A great idea, surely, but Craig reported that in his recent playtests, the birds weren't getting spooked, no matter how much noise he made. Patrick had implemented the bird-scattering code and was positive it was working. He responded, with mock horror, 'I disbelieve!'

It would be amazing, Craig said, if the game could remember how respectful you'd been to the ecosystem, then subtly punish you if you'd trampled too many bees or spooked too many birds, maybe by making subsequent levels slightly more difficult. That would be awesome, Patrick responded, but this Jerk Mode would be a lot of work to implement. He noted that they should instead perhaps focus on more pressing issues, like the fact that time wasn't passing in a linear fashion in recent builds – that players would suddenly plunge into night, or enjoy an endless sunrise. 'Yes,' Craig responded, 'but what is our *concept* for nighttime?' Like a true Nabokovian artist, he was building a world in which he could control everything, from the strength of gravity to the dilation of time. He could also invest all of these things with meaning. 'Right now, nighttime is a bummer. So what is our concept?'

The shadowing session I remember most clearly took place on the morning of April 13th, 2015. Discussion that day focused on how to create the right atmosphere in Ground Control. Craig spoke about it as a place of refuge: a quotidian, comfortable, protected space, away from the dangers and novelties of the alien world, the one place on this planet that the characters had made for themselves, on their own terms, in their own way. As multimedia storytellers, they would need to create that sense of home through words, sounds, music, 3D objects, and movement.

All of this sounded very exciting until they got down to the business of actually doing it. They started with the game's dialogue system: a ten-minute discussion about which controller buttons to assign to what dialogue action. They turned to sounds, pulling up an incomprehensibly massive spreadsheet showing every 'audio asset' they needed (the sound of a heartbeat, a dropped piece of paper, heavy slow footsteps, light fast footsteps, medium medium footsteps), as well as where it needed to happen, whether it had been created yet by their musical collaborator Andy, and whether it had been implemented. (In my notes for that day, around this part of the conversation, having written nothing for nearly an hour, I wrote, 'I haven't fallen asleep. It's just that this is a very boring discussion.')

Next they talked about the shape of the building. Craig was drawing it in a 3D modelling program called Maya but having a hard time getting it to transfer into Unity, the program in which they were building the game. Patrick did some Googling and discovered that the key to the problem was something called an FBX Importer. For over twenty minutes, they walked one another through online tutorials for using the FBX Importer. Nothing was working. After a while, I had to go, and I didn't have the heart to interrupt their discussion about the FBX Importer (Patrick, frustrated, was asking a mute and unhelpful tutorial, 'What? What? What? What?'), so I just hung up, resigning myself to a life of always having to wonder – never to know for certain – if and how and when they finally managed to resolve their FBX problems.

If the problem with *Interstellar* was its lack of grounding, there was no risk of that in game development, where every concept, every wild idea or consciousness-altering interaction, needed to be grounded in a system, an audio asset, a 3D object. A videogame is a ruthlessly grounded thing. Making one seemed like way too much work for two people.

Though I had caught a few stray glances of the game in the two years since my first visit to Craig's place and lurking in on their

Skype sessions, I hadn't actually played the thing. In 2015, though, I finally got a build.

In the period since I first met Craig, the scope of the project had come into focus. The idea was always for *The Future* – as the game was then still called – to be huge. It would ideally become a franchise that Craig and Patrick and their players could live in for decades, one episode every couple of years. After an intense initial period of heavy lifting and lore-creation, the promethean labour of world-building would be complete, the universe would be imagined, and they would shift gears into a steady, relatively relaxed downhill glide.

For a while, in early 2014, they were working on a slice of the universe called *Pilot Projects*, set in the 'cradle world,' the planet the characters were escaping from. This episode, which Craig and Patrick were considering releasing for free as a kind of teaser, focused on the period of pilot training, when the future colonists learned how to fly their helijets and were briefed on their mission. After a few months of Craig and Patrick learning how to make a videogame whose vehicles were fun to fly, *Pilot Projects* was abandoned as a standalone project. Focus shifted to *The Far Shore*, the part of the franchise that focused on the initial exploration of the alien planet. Once they'd taken this decision, they spent the rest of 2014 dividing *The Far Shore* into a five-act structure and building up scattered scenes from that structure. The deal was that if they hadn't figured out how to integrate a big idea by the end of that year, it was out. From the first day of 2015 onward, their focus was squarely on turning all these ideas and systems into a game.

Getting an early build is a great honour and a veritable triumph in the secretive and hyper-observed world of videogames. When a hotly anticipated game is in development – even in development hell – fans dream of getting their hands on an in-progress demo. There's a funny moment in *Indie Game: The Movie* when Edmund McMillen, co-creator of *Super Meat Boy*, imagines the ideal player of his game as an annoying thirteen-year-old version of himself, the kind who would write him obsessively on Twitter, 'Hey, send me a build! My name is Super Meat Boy Fan Boy. I've registered it. I haven't even played the game yet. Get me a demo! C'mon!' No one knew about *The Far Shore*, but if word got out, there would be hundreds of those requests clogging Craig's feed. With a great deal of humility, Craig acknowledged the privileged position I found myself in when he emailed me the Google Drive link to the build.

> so this is a bit of a hasty process but i guess this is also a semi momentous moment?
> or well … this is the first time we've hooked you up with a build, correct?
> fingers crossed it works ok!
> fingers crossed the framerate isnt too rough (it wont be good enough, but i hope it's at least passable here and there)
> fingers crossed there's something in there for you to enjoy or ponder or consider as in progress build

What they sent me were a few episodes from the game's fourth act. Act I was intended as a short, stark, beautiful, spectacular introduction to the aesthetic and themes of the game. In Act II, there would be a bit of gentle action, you'd meet some of the planet's creatures, and you'd establish Ground Control, your home in this unknown world. Act III would be about laying out all the story parameters, getting players acquainted with their flying machines, and teaching them how to survive. Acts IV and V would build on this preparatory work and set players loose in the world to roam, explore, experiment, and subsist.

As a non-gamer and a lover of narrative, Act IV was clearly not the best place for me to jump in. I wanted story and I needed training, which were the province of Acts I–III. But those parts weren't ready yet. Fortunately, I wasn't entirely on my own. In typical Craig fashion, he had sent me ten separate Google Docs – ninety-five pages in total – explaining and walking me through all aspects of the build. I also had ten glorious, uninterrupted days to figure it out while bobbing around the Pacific Ocean.

At roughly the same time as Craig and Patrick were deciding to send me a build, I had decided that, for research purposes, I needed to go to Japan to get to know Patrick better. The game was imminent, after all, and he was half of the creative team responsible for it. I had – through an odd series of events that led to me regularly reviewing cruise vacations for the *Globe and Mail*, Canada's newspaper of record – managed to talk my way into a free return flight to Tokyo, so that I might offer my thoughts on a ten-day trip around Hokkaido. It was a perfect cover: not only would I get a chance to learn more about Patrick than I could get in short bursts of Skype small talk, but I had found my new cruising gig offered a kind of sensory deprivation experience that led to some of the most productive periods in my professional life: not being into shuffleboard, gluttony, or spending an outrageous amount on satellite internet hook-ups, my time at sea gave me plenty of time to reread the works of Tolstoy or Virginia Woolf or Thomas Mann – or explore the vast expanses of *The Far Shore* while recording my observations.

So, on the first morning of my cruise, having breakfasted (and thus exhausted my onboard entertainment options), I settled down with my laptop to read the first document, 'How To Playtest,' which began as follows:

> The build we have this summer is pre-alpha. It's rough and unfinished and it's missing a lot of pieces. We're about a year away from release, we have an awful lot still to do.
>
> On the upside, we're finally in a state where someone not on the project can take a build for a spin, get something out of it, tell us how it's coming across, what's resonating and what isn't, what's confusing and annoying.
>
> It's super essential for us right now to get some solid responses and perspective from other people so we can

gain a better understanding of what we have and how it connects so we can shape things accordingly.

Also! Please do keep the build to yourself. It's our baby we're trusting you with, its unannounced, we aren't looking to invite any unpleasant noise into the process. Thanks for understanding!

I saw right through the humility. It's rough, it's sketchy, it's fundamentally broken – but don't tell anyone about it because it's so awesome that if people found out *how awesome*, all hell would break loose and people wouldn't leave us alone and we'd never finish the game! I decided, with some excitement, to skip the walkthrough for the first segment and just jump right in.

The segment I started with had a cold open: no explanations, no framing, no voices telling me what to do, just me in a helijet. I pressed a few buttons on the controller I had purchased for the occasion and, quickly enough, I was cruising around a three-dimensional landscape. It was a little less abstract than the last time I'd seen it. There was a sea to my left. The water was textured – no crashing waves or anything, but when the sun shone off it, you could see ripples on the surface. It looked okay, but a bit middle-of-the-road. Imagining a visual aesthetic scale that ranged from brutally minimalist and abstract to totally photorealistic, the slider was set dead centre, which felt like a weird place for an indie game to be. Weren't they all about exploring extremes?

Over to my right, there was a rolling green landscape. There were some hills, and from a distance, these had an interesting texture, like lime Jell-O with gold glitter suspended in it. But when I parked my helijet to take a closer look, it became clear that the cool texture was some sort of rendering error that would be smoothed out later in the process: it was just green grass with specks of yellow. I wandered around more, but didn't find much. I returned to my helijet to climb back in, but I couldn't make it work. I pressed all the buttons, but nothing happened. I was trapped in that banal landscape, sliding around like a chess piece.

Sometimes, when I walked by the landing gear of my ship, I passed right through it, like a ghost. After a few minutes of this, I rebooted my computer and started the build again.

My next time through, I stayed in my ship, flying around until I'd seen most of the island, which looked pretty much like a video-game version of an island. The soundtrack that played as I flew was grand, emotional orchestral music – strangely out of step with the action of aimlessly flying around low mountains and a calm sea. Eventually, some instructions appeared on my screen: I was supposed to fly along the coast until I spotted some jellyfish, and then I was supposed to collect ten of them. I looked for the jellyfish but couldn't find anything. Consulting the walkthrough that Craig provided, I saw that I needed to use my 'ping' tool – a tool for non-violently and non-invasively probing the environment for items of interest. After much fumbling with my controller, I figured out how to ping, and I found a jellyfish. It took me so long to finally collect it that I dreaded the process of finding nine more. But I noticed that the jellyfish I'd just collected was still out there on the coastline, impossibly both in my possession and still unclaimed. So I just picked it up nine more times, and in that way completed my mission.

I was told to return to Ground Control. When I figured out how to get back there, I parked my helijet, walked through the airlock, and found myself inside. But that only lasted for a second, because I somehow walked right through a wall and found myself outside again. I walked back through the wall from the outside, and now I was back in Ground Control. I tried to talk to some stick figures, and I got the sense that something really dark was happening, but I couldn't get my controls to work well enough to make anyone tell me precisely what it was. Eventually someone told me to go to my bunk. When I found my way to a dark closet-like space, I was prompted to press the O button to fall asleep. So I did.

They weren't being falsely humble. This was indeed a 'pre-alpha' build. It was rough and unfinished and missing a lot of pieces. If it hinted at greater things to come in the next year, it was beyond my ability to see them. Visually, it was bland, neither here nor there. The music didn't match the action – it seemed like a placeholder. If the idea was to bring together gameplay and narrative, they weren't even close. They had avoided the usual recourse to violence – just give players a bunch of stuff to shoot, and the narrative will fall into place – but the nonviolent tasks they had devised, like picking up ten jellyfish, felt pointless and arbitrary, and they were complicated and boring to carry out. The grand narrative Craig had laid out to me that day in the special room in his house was nowhere to be found, and not even hinted at. I guess I was on the planet that the Tolstoy figure had written about – at one point, I even saw a massive symmetrical mountain in the far distance – but if I hadn't had that talk with Craig, I would just have assumed I was flying around in a simulacrum of rural Japan, maybe on the Tōkaidō, with Mount Fuji in the distance.

As I read on through the walkthrough guides, I saw that Craig and Patrick at least realized the state their game was in: 'This stuff is like 15% complete.' 'The bunkroom will eventually actually look like a bunkroom.' 'We kinda need to get the rest of the game together before we can properly problem solve this woolier stuff.' 'At present it's quite likely the player will not understand the goals, not feel any drama, and not understand how to proceed. So we have our work cut out for us.'

My own work was clearly yet to come. I'd set aside ten days of distraction-free sailing for exploring this early build, but by lunchtime that first day, I was pretty much done. I'd played through a few more scenarios, advancing where I could, interacting where I was able to, walking through a lot of walls and struggling at nearly every turn to make my controller do what I wanted it to. But there wasn't anything for me to dig into, write about, get excited about, or put into context. Not yet. After lunch, I headed up to the ship's library, desperately hoping they'd have something worth reading. I hadn't packed a single book, and there were still nine days of sensory deprivation ahead of me.

Ten days later, I was on a bullet train to Tokyo, en route to meet Patrick, trying to catch glimpses of Mount Fuji in between furiously finishing some academic work I hadn't been able to do on my internet-less cruise. I'd been told by a bunch of people that Mount Fuji was one of those things, like the Grand Canyon, where you think you know what it's going to be like, you've seen a million pictures and you think you're ready for it, but when you see it with your own eyes, it overwhelms you. Despite passing it a few times from a few directions on my visit to Japan, my view had always been completely blocked by clouds – it was my misfortune to come during the rainy season. So every few minutes I would look out the window, and it would be all monochrome foreground: grey factories with cloud behind, off-white apartment buildings with cloud behind, parked silver trains with cloud behind.

But then, suddenly, while lazily looking left, I saw the whole thing, in a flash that lasted a second at most. A corridor opened up between my eyes and the top of Mount Fuji. It was all there: the immense shape, the unnatural symmetry, the unthinkable hugeness, the deep green sides and white tip, with an electric blue sky behind. Then the corridor closed, and the world of pure foreground returned. But that second-long vision stayed with me for the rest of the trip as a reminder of the overwhelming beauty that lies behind everyday experience, that reveals itself suddenly and fully in all its depth and richness, and then is gone.

I met Patrick in the lobby of my hotel. He was sitting on a bench that ran along the outside wall, reading messages on a flip-phone of a kind that, by 2015, was completely obsolete. Even from a distance of twenty or thirty feet, I could see that he was the sort of person it would be easy for me to spend time with. He was quiet and gentle, tall and thin. In a country where everyone is dressed neatly and deliberately, from the salarymen to the Harajuku teens, his clothes were noticeably worn: a pair of long khaki cargo shorts that had been through the wash several hundred times, a threadbare white T-shirt with a logo of the letter P with piano keys sticking out of it and 'perfect piano lesson' written below.

Putting away his anachronistic flip-phone, Patrick pulled out a hand-drawn map and explained our plans for the evening: we would take the Shinjuku line from Shinjuku-sanchome to Sasazuka Station, on the western edge of Shibuya, where we'd get vegetarian ramen and then walk to the indie/hippie neighbourhood of Shimokitazawa, where we would go to a concert. I couldn't help but find the hand-drawn map amusing. Here was the tech-wizard of the game, in the most tech-obsessed city on earth, using a flip-phone and navigating this city's incomprehensible geography – a place whose millions of intertwining streets have no names and buildings have no numbers – with pen and paper.

As we emerged from Sasazuka Station, trying to think of some small talk to head off any enervating discussions of the build, I asked why there were special grooved yellow tiles in the middle of the asphalt sidewalks. I'd noticed them everywhere in the country and couldn't figure out their purpose. Were they like lane lines for pedestrians, sorting the walkers into the proper direction – or to separate bikes from pedestrians? Patrick, who had been in Tokyo for years and spoke fluent Japanese by then, said he didn't know. Maybe they were there to help blind people, he offered.

As we walked toward our ramen, we talked about life in Japan, about how he got into the Japanese indie-music scene, how it led to him meeting his wife. But Patrick was not capable of thinking and talking at the same time, and there was clearly a lot of thinking going on, most of it navigational in nature. The map was a soggy, crumpled mess. I asked him if we were lost, and he said he was just having trouble finding the river he'd drawn on it.

After twenty minutes of walking, we found ourselves in a very quiet neighbourhood, surrounded by low, closely packed houses and a beige elementary school. We asked a man who seemed to be guarding a comically small construction site for directions, but he could offer no help – he wasn't from the area, and only knew how to get back to the train station. We resumed our wandering, Patrick again furiously consulting his hand-drawn map.

As we continued to walk – it had now been forty-five minutes since we'd left the station – I asked Patrick how he felt about living in Japan generally. He really liked it. It is safe and peaceful. The only downside, perhaps, is that there is so much pressure to succeed. I mentioned something about suicide statistics, and he told me that his father-in-law left a lucrative job as an accountant for a large company to switch tracks and become a mental health counsellor. This is an extremely unusual move in Japan, to leave a stable career path to do something uncertain and idealistic. I said that this sounded a lot like leaving a stable job at Koei to start working on an independent videogame, shortly after the birth of a child. He said maybe, but he couldn't have done it without the support of his Japanese family. He, his wife, and his daughter lived with them, and they gave him a large room in their house to use as an office, in a country where space is at a premium.

Just as Patrick completed this story, we arrived at a big subway station. It looked familiar. It was Sasazuka Station, the same place we'd started from. 'I see what happened,' Patrick said. 'We left out the west exit but I thought it was the east. The streets were almost perfect mirror images of one another on either side, so I got all turned around, and it took me a while to realize what was up. But, okay, here, it's this way.'

It was hard not to see a metaphor.

Once we finally got our bearings, our trip went off without a hitch. Patrick's map was barely legible by this point, but it did the job. He found the river, which led us to the vegetarian ramen place, a truly tiny spot with seating for about six. When we were done, we followed an incident-free route down to Shimokitazawa, briefly checking out its mildly bohemian main street (much tie-dye on display) before ducking into a small alley to look for the Shimokitazawa Era, the club that was our destination. This was an important spot, Patrick informed me. Although I had picked it somewhat randomly from a massive list of options he'd emailed in advance of my visit, it was his favourite club in all Tokyo. In fact, it was in this very place that he had seen his first Tokyo indie show, perfect piano lesson, the band from his T-shirt, way back in his first days in the city.

Shimokitazawa Era looked like no indie rock club I'd ever seen. There was no line of leather-jacketed fans crushing cigarettes under their Converse high-tops. In fact, there was no one outside at all, and no obvious signs that this was even a club. The building looked like a dentist's office, four floors of anonymous beige tile. The club was on the top floor, with no natural light and every surface painted black. Someone who called himself a rapper told jokes – or so Patrick told me – to a crowd of eight, who did at least appear to be laughing. As the evening progressed, it became clear we were the only people in the room who weren't on the bill.

When the rapper finished, the guys on the left got up and played a set of polished pop-punk. They would have been fine playing in a stadium. They had walk-up music! They did choreographed lunges and pirouettes! The heroin-chic lead singer winked at me coquettishly before diving into a chorus! Amazing showmanship for an audience of two. If I hadn't randomly selected their show from Patrick's list, would they have bothered playing?

When they finished, two hippies got up. They were an 'effetor band' – a guitar, one of those keyboards with a little clear hose that you blow into, and lots of effects pedals – and they were absolutely horrible, out of time with one another and unskilled in a way that was exasperating. At one point, one of the keys on the blow-keyboard died; the blow-keyboardist gave an apologetic speech and they trundled offstage. (Patrick leaned over to me and summarized the situation: 'Apparently the key that broke corresponded to a very important note.')

Finally, three women in flowy outfits – the headliners, retolighter – took the stage. They too were a bit of a mess from a technical perspective, but at least they were having fun. Every song was in a different genre: one recalled Japanese festival music, another was pop-punk, another shoegaze. In their thrilling last song, it was like each *instrument* was playing in a different genre – festival music drumming with Blink-182 bass and My Bloody Valentine guitar. It was a performance that captured a lot of what I like best about the DIY ethic of punk. They weren't very good at their instruments, but they weren't letting that stop them from having a good time together, expressing themselves, putting on a show. As a result, they sounded like no one else, they were utterly themselves, and they gave us an experience we couldn't have had anywhere else. They weren't taking themselves too seriously, either on stage or in person, as they made clear when they came and sat down with us briefly after their show, laughing with Patrick about how bad they were, how awful the show was, how embarrassing it was that no one came – and we protested that we'd loved them, that we'd never forget their performance or this night, and we hoped they'd always remember the night they played a private show for two foreigners in their thirties.

We left the club and I said goodbye to Patrick. It was 10:30 p.m., and the train back to where he lived, on the other side of Tokyo, would stop running soon. Alone once again, my thoughts returned to the messiness of DIY art – and the messiness of my own theories about it. For me, the night's show had been an undisputed success – I knew right away that I would always think of it as one of the best concerts I'd ever seen. But if you tried to evaluate it according to the rubrics of riot grrrl or the Hogarth Press, you would have to declare it a failure: retolighter weren't trying to change the world, they weren't extending the distribution of the sensible, and they had only barely reached any audience at all. It struck me that if the game came out and met a similar fate – a brilliant shambles, a colourful wreck, with an audience of zero – everyone would consider it a failure. Certainly, it would be a disaster for Craig and Patrick and their families: all that wasted time, effort, and money. But if it presented something genuinely new, something really daring and honest, I wouldn't hold failure against it. If anything, failure would only make me love it more.

The next day, I was sitting in Patrick's home office, a fresh note-book in hand. After introducing me to his family, he'd arranged two chairs by his desk, and we sat in a slightly awkward silence. We'd both understood that yesterday was for getting to know one another, and today was for getting down to business.

'So, what did you think of the build?' he finally asked.

I could see right away that he knew what I'd say, that I was disappointed. So I just told him exactly how I felt. The gameplay was clumsy and boring. The visual style was bland. The music seemed overblown – the only way I could cultivate any tension was by muting the soundtrack and playing Wire's *Chairs Missing* on my iPhone. I was worried that the game was in fact regressing, becoming more 'normal' and thus less interesting.

Patrick nodded along. He said he was disappointed too. Most of the things I was talking about – visual style, flair, music – weren't really his province as a systems/programming guy, but he felt them, too. The game wasn't grabbing him. He was worried it was getting out of control. A huge story. A bunch of characters. Tons of dialogue. Not only flying a ship, but also walking around. 'We've got a big mess on our hands,' he said. The playtest notes had said they hoped to ship within a year, but Patrick nodded when I said that seemed extremely optimistic.

He said he wanted to show me something. In May 2011, right before he moved to Tokyo for good, Patrick was in Toronto work-ing at Koei Canada when Craig invited him out for brunch. *Sworcery* had just come out at the end of March, but Craig was already thinking of the next project. *Sworcery* had made Craig a lot of money, and it would surely make him more. This meant that he could plan his next steps in a very deliberate way, in his own manner and at his own pace. At that moment, over brunch in May 2011, that meant total independence, total control over the schedule and pre-release hype, and working with a tiny team of people he really liked. His dream team was three people: him, Patrick, and his musician friend Andy Rohrmann, a.k.a. scntfc. He asked Patrick if he would like to try out this partnership over the course of the upcoming 'game jam,' TOJam, where game creators get together and challenge one another to make something cool under brutal time constraints. It was the same event where, in 2009, Craig had produced the quasi-demo for *Sworcery* called *Alpinist*.

Patrick agreed, and over the course of that three-day weekend, they made a prototype for *The Far Shore* called *Rootdown*. It was cobbled together completely from scratch. They weren't working in an established game engine like Unity – it was just written in C++ with a few libraries. The experience was incredibly compressed and unbelievably successful. At the end of the weekend, Patrick could only marvel at what they'd created. It was a perfect mashup of *Fatal Inertia* and *Sworcery*, a moody, stylish, arty, three-dimensional flying game that somehow suggested mystery and mythology. Patrick knew that when the opportunity came, he'd quit what he was doing to work on this project. Two years later, he did.

As he told me the backstory, he rooted around in the DOS prompt for a copy of *Rootdown*. He hadn't played it in years. He'd been so focused on making the game that *Rootdown* unleashed that he'd half-forgotten it existed. At the time, there had been some talk of releasing *Rootdown* as a kind of early teaser – that's how amazing it had been and how confident they'd felt after that weekend. But that fizzled out, and as a result, very few people had even seen it. It existed now only as a bunch of sketchy builds on Patrick's hard drive, none of which, that day in Tokyo, seemed to be working. But finally, after many failed attempts, many instances in which his current configuration of software and hardware refused to execute commands it had been more than happy to obey in the distant past of May 2011, he found a version that worked. It was stunning.

The concepts were familiar. There was a funny-looking pixellated little ship, a helijet. There was a mountainous landscape. You flew the ship through the landscape and tried to get to a particular spot, and then flew around to achieve some other oblique purpose, and then it was over in a few minutes, without your realizing what you'd really done.

Somehow it was a blissful experience. The colours were bold and loud – pinks, oranges, dazzling blues and purples. The mountains were abstract and jagged – totally unlike real mountains, way too tall and spiky, and so able to convey that sense of wonder at the unfamiliar, the weird and compelling. The music was strange too, angular and a little off, noisy and fast and broken-feeling. Watching that ending bit of gameplay, whatever the hell was happening – Patrick was flying the ship in circles around a central column; great huge shafts of light would descend when he did the right thing, the whole screen would shake when he did something wrong – I wanted to try it. Even I, with my shitty gaming skills, wanted to see if I could summon those shafts of light.

As Patrick finished up the demo, he looked over at me. His huge smile turned slowly into a massive sigh. In that moment, it was obvious to both of us. They had made *Rootdown* in three days, in a completely hacky, intuitive, amateurish way. And yet this little game was infinitely better than the thing they'd been working on rigorously, assiduously, deliberately for the past two years.

8.

Inevitably, the game did not come out in 2016, as the Coach House catalogue had promised. After this failure to launch, during the historical period that Jesper Juul calls the 'indiepocalypse,' the project settled into a new rhythm. We agreed, that the next build I would see would be the beta – that is, a game that is pretty much ready to go. (This wouldn't arrive until July 2021.) In the meantime, Craig and I had yearly epic Skype chats. Our meetings were seldom very encouraging: he and Patrick seemed to be working on the same things they'd been working on the previous year, the screenshots he shared look distressingly familiar, distressingly like the prototype I'd played in 2015. Although they had plans for how to proceed, their belief in these plans seemed to be evaporating. Whenever my publisher emailed for updates, with decreasingly optimistic subject lines, I replied with some variation of 'I'm still in touch with them – but, yeah, no idea.'

In our yearly chats in this middle period, I always got the sense that Craig was trying to put on a brave face in a difficult situation. He'd start by showing me Google Docs with deadlines and milestones, as if I were an investor, like he was trying to convince me my money was in good hands, that everything was plausibly on track. There's a mechanic in the finished version of *JETT* whereby conversation proceeds by your asking other characters about either their 'Mood' or their 'Task.' Craig was always squarely focused on 'Task' for the first part of our conversations. I'd just listen patiently, not always understanding all the details, given my foggy sense of the nitty-gritty of videogame production and my lack of a recent build to compare his reflections against.

But then, sometime in the second or third or fourth hour of our chat, the needle would shift from 'Task' to 'Mood,' and I would get an honest accounting of his emotional state. By 2017 – the halfway point of the project, as it turned out, four years in, four more to go – his mood was manifestly grim. Work had shifted from deciding what they wanted to make to figuring out how they were actually going to make it, and any sense of excitement in the concepts of the game – its lore, its vibe, its narrative, its potential to impact the culture – had vanished. He described the stages of the project to me as follows: (1) 'What feelings do we want to summon?' to (2) 'Okay, we're committed to *these* feelings,' to (3) 'How are we going to summon those feelings, pragmatically?' to (4) 'How are we going to do it within the time we're giving ourselves?' It was 'a move toward pragmatic production, which then sort of replaces the wonderment.' He was not enjoying this shift – and 'pragmatic production' was not turning out to be a strength. The enormity of the task of making an ambitious video-game with a team of two people was revealing itself with increasing clarity. In one of our conversations, I mentioned that I'd been reading some of the half-serious agitprop plays that W. H. Auden and Christopher Isherwood had written together in the 1930s. He asked some questions about their process, then compared it to his and Patrick's:

It's a bit like, two playwrights get together, write a bunch of scenes for a *Pirates of the Caribbean*–like roller coaster ride. And they have to be there during the construction of the animatronic robots. And then they actually have to *build* the animatronic robots – actually become roboticists. They have to ensure the safety of the roller coaster, make sure that the loop-de-loops are exciting enough … And then, at the end, if the dialogue is wooden in one of the scenes, that's still on them.

It was not only that there was so much to do and that everything took so long ('You can spend two days on *just a frog*,' he told me, 'and the frog's still not done. But you sure did spend those two days'). It was also that they weren't sure exactly what they should be doing at a given moment. 'In my heart of hearts, I know we've made bad decisions,' he told me in 2017. 'I don't know where exactly, but I know there's a lot of them.' The sense of passing time was weighing on him, as was a growing sense of misalignment between JETT time and real-world time.

> There's the frustration of 'What friggin year is it and I'm still not done and I want to move on and I want to do a thing with the house but I can't until this happens?' […] Kids are growing up. The world is changing. We're all getting closer to where we're headed. And I'm still just doing this thing over here.

Compounding the time problem was the familiar worry that, in the midst of the indiepocalypse, even if they could make the game they had in their heads, its moment had already passed. 'Reports from the landscape out there are not positive,' he said in 2017:

> It seems like *Sworcery* kind of got in toward the end of that first era [for indie games], and now we're sort of post–that era. Since 2012, the numbers paint an incredibly bleak picture, where what should be a notable high-quality project just goes off a cliff and nobody notices.

Imagining the future made him even more anxious than focusing on the difficulties they were facing in the present.

> What if I look back at these as the golden times because I didn't yet know we flopped? We get to launch and it goes out and it flops and then you have to figure out the rest of your life. And you look back at those years when I was just mildly anxious and think, "*those* were the years!" … Personally, there's a shame that I can't do this better and can't solve this faster.'

But there was nothing to do but keep going. 'I'm aware of how absurd this is and I'm frustrated by it,' he told me by way of apology for the frustrations he was causing me and my publishing trajectory. 'But I can't think of a way out of it except to proceed.'

One concrete way to move forward was to bring in help. From the start, Craig, Patrick, and Andy knew they didn't possess all the skills to complete a major videogame. In 2013, Craig was an artist with some experience on a few games, but not much in 3D. Patrick had worked on big games and had ideas about design, but his role was that of a programmer, the guy who built the stuff, not the one who decided what would be built. Andy was a musician who released his own records and worked in film and TV and had contributed exactly one song to exactly one videogame: *Sworcery*.

They hired a few people in limited ways during the middle years, most notably the environment artist Flaminia Grimaldi, who stayed on the project to the end and played a big role. But bringing people on was tricky for at least two reasons. First, good people are expensive. Second, getting them up to speed on the project was, as Craig explained it, 'just a nightmare': 'Here's our Google Drive, there's a million documents, it will take you a day and a half to piece any of it together, and here's footage, and here's builds.' As such, when they encountered something they didn't know how to do, they mostly tried to learn how to do it themselves.

As the project advanced, it became clear that the core team had two main weaknesses, which no amount of bootstrapping could overcome: game design and production. The role of a game designer is to make the game play *well* – to ensure that the player always knows what they're doing and is having fun. 'Craig and I don't have the greatest design chops,' Patrick told me: they could make things pretty, make them work, wrap them up in swaths of lore, but they weren't the best at making it clear what a repair kit was, how to assemble one, or why you needed to do it now. And they definitely weren't succeeding at making any of this *fun*. (All of this was certainly clear to me when I played the build they sent me in the summer of 2015).

What a game designer does for players in the game, a producer does for the people making the game. They set the schedule, manage the budget, and make sure everyone knows what they're doing and check that they do it. (In an ideal world, everyone has fun, too.) Although they tried very hard, Craig and Patrick also obviously lacked production skills. During one of our mid-period Skype calls, Craig showed me a massive spreadsheet he'd been working on, an attempt to get a handle on production. It was so massive, so Borgesian in its complexity, that it was obviously doing more harm than good. One part of the spreadsheet tallied up the estimated time that each member of the team still had to put into the project. For Craig, the number was 1,223.021 hours. (Despite its many-decimalled precision, it was way off: by my own estimate, the number at that point – about halfway – was more like 15,000).

When I spoke to him in the summer of 2017, our conversation focused on how badly they needed production and design help, how the core team had hit a dead end, run out of cards to play. Six years in, it was too late to have a game designer come in and rebuild things from the ground up – but they desperately needed someone to at least steer them toward the least-worst solutions to the various intractable gameplay knots they were stuck in. 'We've been on this thing forever. We've talked about every idea ever. So we approach a problem we've approached before and there are nine good ideas, and we've lost the conviction to say, "This is the one we've gotta go with." We need someone to come in and say, "Well, from my perspective, this dot connects to that dot."' Given the budget constraints, it would be helpful if this same person also understood production – could find the solutions that made the game fun *and* finishable. What they needed was an 'old wizard guiding us out of the forest': 'He doesn't need to be there all the time, he just needs to say, "This way!"' Reflecting on this moment later in the process, he described their situation in 2017: 'We had the whole thing there, but it was unfinished. How do you hike it to the finish line? You really do need a designer and a producer with expertise.'

The first move was to reach out to respected industry veterans, set them up with a build and some design documents, and see what they thought. It's a testament to the respect Craig enjoys among his peers that he was able to put together such an indie-game all-star team: Chris Bell, who had previously worked on *Journey* and at that time was in the midst of shipping *What Remains of Edith Finch*; Nels Anderson of *Firewatch* and *Mark of the Ninja*; and Kent Hudson, whose resume includes titles in the *Thief* and *Deus Ex* franchises, and who, like Anderson, was thanked on the credits of *Gone Home*. All provided helpful feedback, but none had the bandwidth for anything but a one-off consultation. Kent Hudson had a suggestion, however: the person Craig and Patrick really needed for this, the old wizard they sought, was Randy Smith.

I'd been hearing about Randy for years, but I didn't actually get a chance to speak with him until late summer of 2021, when his role on the game was mostly complete. The day before Randy and I were scheduled to meet, I was chatting with Craig and Patrick, who suggested I check out a Noclip documentary about the making of the pioneering stealth game *Thief*, which, they said, contained essential footage of a young Randy Smith. The documentary chronicles the late-nineties/early-aughts glory days of the brilliantly ramshackle Boston videogame studio Looking Glass, full of untidy MIT-trained geniuses working ungodly hours to produce genre-defining titles that the public never quite understood. When Randy is introduced about halfway into the film, he immediately stands out from his indifferently groomed colleagues, with their unkempt beards, frizzy ponytails, and ill-fitting hoodies. This old wizard is no Gandalf. His blond hair cut like Tony Hawk's, dressed in a billowy, shimmering, retina-punching silky red shirt unbuttoned over a T-shirt with a huge five-pointed star, his look is iconically late-nineties alternative – but you'd take him for the frontman in a slacker band, a character in a Richard Linklater film, a clerk in an underground comics shop, not a guy working on a videogame. When I met Randy the next day, twenty years after he worked on *Thief*, the details were a bit different – a maroon V-neck T-shirt replacing red silk, the hair a little longer, combed in a dramatic swoosh across his forehead. Yet the vibe was the same: a charismatic, self-assured boy genius, a perfect nineties vision of a cool dude.

Randy grew up around games. Pong systems hit homes the year he was born. His family was into board and card games, and he was eight when he started programming and making games of his own on an old Commodore VIC-20. He had all the consoles: Nintendo, PlayStation, whatever. When he went to college, there were no game-design programs, but he inadvertently created one of his own, studying computer science and media arts. His first job was with Looking Glass, a studio renowned for game design in particular, and it functioned like videogame grad school. In the following years, he designed and directed games in the *Thief* series, worked on the never-to-be-released Steven Spielberg video-game LMNO, and co-founded his own indie studio, Tiger Style, which released three games – *Spider: The Secret of Bryce Manor* (2009), *Waking Mars* (2012), and *Spider: Rite of the Shrouded Moon* (2015) – before shutting down. (It is worth mentioning here that although I keep attributing the term 'indiepocalypse' to Jesper Juul, Randy Smith was on the GDC 2016 panel where the term was actually coined.)

In 2017, Randy found himself 'in between gigs.' He had an idea for a game he wanted to make but wasn't in a position to start just yet. In the meantime, he was taking on consulting work. From a mailing list came news that Superbrothers was looking for help with ecosystems on their new game. Kent Hudson got in touch with Randy and told him the same thing he had told Craig: he'd be a perfect fit. Randy knew Craig from game festivals: the first *Spider* was an iOS game and had been up for some of the same awards as *Sworcery*. He didn't know Patrick, but Patrick knew him: Looking Glass games were a huge part of Patrick's childhood, and he was a big fan of *Waking Mars*. (Indeed, during a Skype in 2016, long before any professional contact with Randy, Patrick guiltily admitted he was borrowing a few ideas from *Waking Mars* for JETT.) They all met and decided to work together.

Initially, Randy's involvement was, as he put it to me, 'very peripheral.' This was mostly for financial reasons: although Craig considered Randy's role critical to the success of the project, they just didn't have the funds to bring him on in a major way. 'Even part-time overstates it,' Craig said, 'because we only had what was left over in the Superbrothers bank, so every Randy hour was treated with a lot of care.' Randy's role, at the start, was multifaceted but necessarily arm's-length: he looked at that massive production spreadsheet and various design documents, he played through whatever builds they had, and he provided feedback. His job was not to steer the overall direction of the project but to bring the granular details in line with the grand vision. As Craig told me shortly after Randy joined the project, the kinds of questions they were asking him were 'Should this button do this, or should the frog jump left or jump right?' 'He doesn't touch the big concepts,' he told me, 'unless they're getting in the way of that stuff.'

Randy's initial impression was that the project 'knew what it wanted to be,' but 'was faltering.' The DNA was very clear. It had a story, a world, an aesthetic, characters, a particular feeling of flight. 'The spirit was really there,' Randy said. But the absence of an experienced game designer in the team was apparent. 'When I arrived at the project,' Randy told me, 'there was an enormous black hole where a game designer would have been working for all the years these guys had been working on the project.' There was definitely material there: there were controls, terrain, jet manoeuvres, concepts for materials like vapour. 'But the game systems, like, "Oh, when this happens and this number changes to this and the player should be thinking this way"' – the 'mechanics that react to each other to track what the player is doing and update [their] notion of success or failure' – were in a poor state. '"Rudimentary,"' Randy said, 'would be a great compliment.'

From his arm's-length consulting role, he could only react to what the team were producing: 'I don't know if a person is going to understand this,' or 'I don't feel engaged by this mechanic, it needs to be a credible threat.' What they needed was someone working full-time to proactively identify and to solve JETT's many game design problems. 'And no one was doing that' – until, that is, the Sony money came through, Randy happened to be available, and they were able to bring him on full-time.

By the end of 2018, it was clear they couldn't just proceed as they had been – that drastic change was needed. As bleak as things felt and looked in 2017, Craig would later see 2018 as the emotional nadir of the project. It was the peak season for what Craig termed 'existential dread.'

The main development was that he was running out of money. That year, it was 'just us churning away, bringing on little contributors here and there, churning away – and the money that *Sworcery* made had been going down as the years went by.' Patrick's war chest was diminishing, too. Questions that had been in the background or relegated to night thoughts now needed to be confronted directly in the light of day: 'How on earth are we going to get this done? *Are* we going to get this done? And even if we were to get it done, what would that look like? Is there a chance that we just took all of our money over seven or eight years, put it in a hole, and then that's it, that's the end of the story?' He began actively considering contingency plans – what was his wife's salary looking like? What backup did he have if he didn't know how to finish this game? 'As 2018 became 2019 and I could see the bottom of the Superbrothers bank,' he said, 'that sort of existential dread was weighing heavily.'

In the depths of this despair, when things were at their bleakest, a column of light finally opened. At precisely this moment, Craig happened to catch up with his old friend Mark MacDonald, a

Tokyo-based industry videogame veteran. When I'd visited Japan in 2015, Craig had hoped we'd be able to meet up, but Mark was busy getting married. Back then, he was hosting an influential podcast and working at a studio that translated English games into Japanese and had localized *Sworcery* for the Japanese market. In the years since, Mark had been leading what Craig called 'flaw-less' PR and strategy campaigns at Enhance Games, for titles like *Tetris Effect* and *Rez Infinite*. Craig explained his predicament to Mark. Mark, in turn, described a plausible way out. Going into this conversation, Craig later told me,

> I thought we had to just hike it to the finish and throw it into the market and just cross our fingers and hope that we can support our families. But it turns out that there's this secret finish line that you can hit, like a year before launch, where you can have that relief – and still have that anticipation of really wanting to knock it out of the park and everything like that – but to have resolved a lot of those anxieties early.

The 'secret finish line' was the world of platform deals, which work as follows. Platforms – consoles like Xbox, PlayStation, and Nintendo Switch – are in competition with one another, and one way that they can gain a competitive advantage is by having exclusive content. So they are always looking for interesting games and studios, eager to exchange cash for exclusivity to their plat-form. In general, these deals are done about a year out from launch, and the game studios use the cash to fund the expensive final stages of production. The deal works like an advance in publishing: when the game comes out, the platform uses sales to recoup their investment in the game; but if it flops and never makes back its advance, the developers don't have to pay the plat-form back – the cash is theirs to keep. Thus, the resolution of anxieties. If you can secure such a deal – and if you've been smart enough to include back salaries into your budget, paying yourself for all the work you've put into the game to that point, not 'cartoon money,' but a reasonable amount – then even if the game doesn't sell a single copy, it's okay, you've been paid sensibly for your work, you haven't thrown your life savings into a hole. Also, when you pay contributors to help you finish things up, the money's coming out of the platform's pocket, not the Superbrothers bank.

Not only was the idea appealing – a *deus ex machina* solution to existential dread – but the timing was perfect. That's because in 2019 – the very year that Jesper Juul published *Handmade Pixels*, which classed the post-2015 period as the 'indiepocalypse' – the indiepocalypse ended. It was all due to the platforms. Partly it was because a new generation of consoles was on the horizon. In early 2019, the PS5 and Xbox Series X hadn't yet been announced, but rumours were circulating, and the big manufacturers were looking for games to entice players to upgrade. Platform wars were also stirring in the PC and mobile markets. In December 2018, Epic Games, riding high on the mega-success of *Fortnite*, launched a PC gaming platform to compete with Valve's Steam. In March 2019, Apple announced their Arcade videogame subscription service. At the same time, Google was developing their rival mobile platform, Stadia, which launched in November. The owners of these platforms included some of the largest companies on earth: Valve (worth about $10 billion), Epic Games ($30 billion), Sony ($250 billion), Google ($1.5 trillion), Microsoft and Apple ($2 trillion apiece). They were all looking for content. As Craig breathlessly explained to me in the summer of 2019,

There's never been a moment like this in the industry before, where you have these big tech players like Google or Microsoft or Epic – they want your cool game to be on their platform and they're willing to take money that they got from *Fortnite* or Google ad revenue or whatever these piles of money that these giants have – they're willing to take some of that just for the privilege of having your game on their platform. And it's just a seller's market. So it's a weird situation where money grows on trees in a way that it typically does not.

Andy Rohrmann, who during the long development process for JETT worked on music for lots of other games, was feeling it too. It was a 'secondary boom' for indies and small studios, he told me. Companies like Apple and Google that had previously merely paid attention were now actively fostering and financing projects large and small. At the start of 2019, 'five times the amount of money started flowing in, gold-rush style.'

Wanting to be part of the gold rush, eager to pluck some of this money suddenly growing on trees, Craig started strategizing. He talked to Mark, he got in touch with Mark's friend Ryan Payton, an industry veteran who was running his own successful studio, Camouflaj, and he teamed up with Popagenda, a Montreal-based firm that provides production, development, and PR support to small studios. They told him he needed a budget for his 'ask,' some number that would pay him and Patrick for all their work to that point and fund the work that remained. He also needed to put together a 'pitch deck' for potential partners. He researched all the platforms that might be interested, then started reaching out. It was quickly apparent that *everyone* wanted to meet, that he'd have his choice of suitors. As Craig's brother Mack later explained it to me, 'There's just enough medium-level videogame mogul intellectuals in the space that have such a soft spot for the game [*Sworcery*] and the brand [Superbrothers] that you could totally come in and meet with x, y, z.'

A trip would be necessary – to the Bay Area, of course. Plans came together quickly. Craig bought his plane ticket the week before leaving. Having previously always stayed with friends when he visited the area, he booked his first ever San Francisco hotel room. It was a real business trip: 'This was my first at-bat as a bizdev guy with a slideshow.' He arrived on a Sunday, just after that year's Game Developers Conference had wrapped up. He had meetings scheduled for Monday, Tuesday, and Wednesday.

On the receiving end of the slide show – x, y, and z – would be Sony, Google, and Apple.

Although the pitch was tailored to suit the individual platform, it went more or less as follows. First up was a two-minute video clip that focused solely on emotion and mood, leaving out any glimpse of actual gameplay. It was remarkably like the trailer they showed more than a year later at the PS5 launch event: the curtains of a yurt open onto a dreamy steppe landscape, you say goodbye to your parents, head off into a jett, get a look at your comrades in the cosmodrome, then launch off into the unknown. Next up in the pitch deck were ten minutes' worth of slides explaining the vision and backstory of the project, laying out its core mechanics, presenting a timeline for completion, and explaining what the team needed to get their project across the finish line. Finally, four minutes of gameplay footage that, again, was startlingly like the second *JETT* trailer, released in July 2021. Characters, dialogue, landscape, and jett movement – all showed the need for a bit of polish, but were otherwise identical to the actual gameplay of the finished product. (Craig and Patrick weren't exaggerating when they say that the fundamentals were all in place before the big platform deals got done – at least in terms of what could be fit into a heavily curated clip.)

Where the slide deck departed from the finished product was in terms of tone. Although Craig initially framed *JETT* in direct opposition to *Sworcery* – no pixels, no irony, no hipstery language, no manifestos – its vocabulary and audiovisual iconography were all over the pitch. The emotion clip started the same way *Sworcery* does, with the beam-down sound effect. The tone of the slides was arch in a way that *JETT* decidedly is not. One slide described the project as 'a narrative-driven action adventure game with substance, style, depth and breadth set within a fresh science fiction psycho-cosmology' – the latter quasi-Jungian term coming straight out of the Archetype's mouth. Listing a series of videogame and sci-fi inspirations, one slide read, 'likely some vibes in common here.' Laying out some of the game's complex mythology, which reads as dark and dire in the finished game, another slide said, 'for people who like intricate lore & mysteries & meta-textual cosmic weirdness, we have good news.' The final slide listed Craig's contact information, then concluded in *Sworcery*'s characteristic hipster-slacker style, 'thx for this chit chat!' In crafting the presentation to evoke the mood, the vibes, the cosmic weirdness of *Sworcery*, Craig was being pragmatic, showing his awareness of what got him in the room. It worked.

The first meeting was with Sony. Craig and Geneviève St-Onge from Popagenda headed out from downtown San Francisco to San Mateo, where the reception was warm and the slideshow went over well. One of the executives in the meeting told Craig it was the best presentation they'd seen in ages, and followed that up with, 'I don't know if it was your plan to only release a game every ten years, but I'll tell you what, your timing is perfect.' Perfect not only in the secondary indie boom, platform-wars macro sense, but also in terms of the micro scale of weeks and days. If they had come the week before, during GDC, they would have been one of 200 games Sony saw, and Sony wouldn't have had time to process their competitors' platform announcements, made during the conference. By the time Craig and Gen arrived, Sony had their marching orders, and it was obvious to everyone in the room that *JETT* was a perfect fit.

The next day, a Tuesday, Craig headed with Ryan Payton to visit Google in Embarcadero. This was the meeting he was least excited about, mostly because of the way that Stadia was being tied to another Google platform, YouTube, about which Craig had deep reservations. There were the connections to Gamergate and to the broader 'shadow universe' of pizzagate conspiracy theorists. The Christchurch mosque shootings had just happened when Craig arrived in the Bay Area, and just before carrying out the attacks, the gunman had said to the camera, 'Remember, lads, subscribe to PewDiePie,' a YouTuber known mostly for his let's-play videos. By that point, Craig told me, 'I won't allow my kids anywhere near YouTube.' Taking money from Google to complete his beloved and high-minded passion project – 'with Stadia rolling out, and Stadia being so close to YouTube, and YouTube having all this baggage…' – just didn't seem to make sense. Craig felt so positive about the Sony meeting that he decided to put his cards on the table and raise his reservations about YouTube. He asked whether Google planned to use the Stadia launch as an opportunity to 'reset YouTube' and 'more muscularly grapple' with its various entrenched catastrophes. The people he was meeting with – dev relations people in the videogame space – weren't exactly in a position to reset YouTube. Still, 'they didn't muster much of a response.'

The last meeting, on the Wednesday, was with Apple. It took place in Apple's then-new headquarters, Apple Park, the circular structure that had already become known as 'the spaceship.' Understandably for a guy neck-deep in a decade-long development process for a videogame named after a spaceship, Craig was distracted by the architecture. 'It was a treat to me, just to see how absurd that thing is,' he said. 'You could feel Steve Jobs' … *insanity* in every corner.' The space was totally disorienting, a huge circle with no signage, no colours, nothing to distinguish one part from any other, every section 'identical … *identical.*' The decor was 'Starfleet bland.' There were coffee shops in every 'wedge,' but they had no signs; you ordered from an app. Everything had been custom-built to conform to the rounded shapes: 'It's all designed to be as impersonal and expensive as possible.' And yet it was totally impractical: they'd forgotten to soundproof the boardrooms, there was insufficient parking, there was apparently no daycare facility. 'They did an impossible, beautiful, incredible thing … but *why* did they do it?' he reflected. 'It did not disappoint. It was such a treat, all the foibles.' (The fact that Craig – neck-deep in a decade-long development process for a beautiful, incredible, maybe impossible thing – was so impressed by Apple Park, so enthralled with its foibles, is worth noting.)

As to the meeting itself, it went well. Craig met with twelve Apple employees in one of their non-soundproofed boardrooms, gave his presentation, and was met with strong interest. There were many hurdles: the specs for the Apple Arcade devices – phones and tablets – were lower than consoles, so it would be tricky to make the controls touch-based, and the Apple funding model was somewhat bizarre … But there was a meeting of minds, and both sides committed to exploring how it all might work.

Business trip done, Craig packed up his iPad, checked out of his cozy hotel, and returned to the woods. We next spoke in June, three months later, at which point discussions were still ongoing with several potential partners, and were quite advanced with Sony. Reflecting on his trip to the Bay Area with a few months' distance, he had some reservations about the position he found himself in. He had played the role of 'bohemian entrepreneur' to a T, and saw the contradictions in that:

> We're trying to do something honest and meaningful. But you kind of have to step back and say, 'And now we're going to ask a tech giant for money for it, to fit into their catalogue of selling more widgets or whatever. And it's just weird to inhabit both roles. And to be switching back and forth, like 'I'm the businessman wheeling and dealing, and now I have to put that down and try to tune back into the more creative side of it.'

But that June, the dominant emotion was astonished, joyful relief. I never saw Craig so relaxed, so happy, so unguarded, and so in awe of his own good luck.

> We might be finding ourselves on this just completely different trajectory than we imagined. We imagined we'd be just another game – hopefully we launch and hopefully we get money back, and we're just one of the many games that tries to do that. But it seems we might be in this lane where – I don't know if we'll be shot out of a cannon exactly, but we could end up riding this wave of platform launch.

He said it again, barely able to believe it: 'It seems like we're on deck to ride this New PlayStation wave …' He realized there was a lot of work ahead. 'Things are a lot more real going forward. Deadlines will matter. There will be consequences for any slippage. So there's a certain element of, "Put your seat in the upright position, put your tray tables away, and buckle your safety belts because, here we go, we're landing in the next twenty minutes!"' But overall, the feeling was 'wind in our sails for the remaining legs of the journey.'

The next month, Jori threw a big party to celebrate Craig's fortieth birthday: friends came in from Toronto and Montreal, a horse and carriage were rented. The Sony deal still hadn't been signed, but it was getting closer and closer. In August, Craig took his elder daughter, then just turned five, on her first trip to the West Coast, where Craig's parents and siblings all live. While he and his daughter were having lunch in the Vancouver Aquarium, the Sony contract finally came in. He stepped aside for a second to use DocuSign on his phone, and then it was done, a seven-figure deal. A few months later, in November, he signed another seven-figure deal with Epic Games Store.

Looking back on this period a year later, he said, 'Those were exciting times. And what was so exciting about it was that a good part of that existential dread was being lifted. In exchange, new pressures. But those pressures were certainly preferable to the existential dread.'

Time, as ever, would tell.

9.

If the platform deals rescued JETT from one form of dread, they launched it into another. The final phase of the project – from the time the platform cash arrived to the point when the game actually got finished – was dominated by *structural* dread.

When all was said and done, Craig told me, 'I've just been in hell for a lot of this.' 'It was pretty unbearable,' he said: 'I will never put myself in a position like that ever again.' Patrick was on the same page. 'My biggest thing is I never want to work on something that takes that long again.' The source of their dread was structural: the inevitable consequence of an almost completely independent production abruptly ramping up to full-on industrial scale. Two people working mostly alone on a tiny budget suddenly had millions of dollars in their hands, zero experience spending such sums, somewhat naïve faith in the advisors they brought in to help, and inflated expectations regarding this money's magic ability to transform their unfinished game into a shippable product. Craig told me that when they signed the Sony deal, 'There was a feeling of, "Hey, we did it!" Not that it wasn't going to be hard work. But we brought funding in, and we brought experienced people in. And so, things should move forward, not of their own accord, but … *propulsively*. But then, that's just not how it works.'

As Patrick said, 'There was a lot of naïveté about how we ramped up. It was very fast, very loose, and chaotic.' Craig said, 'Every part of this was ad hoc. We're making it up this week, we're making it up next week, because no one has the time to streamline this and say, "It can run more smoothly."'

A major challenge, maybe the main one, was learning how to work with the big team they were putting together. Sam Bradley was one of the first people hired into the expanding team, brought on as art director. As he put it, 'it had just been them and two or three people for so long, and then you try to adapt in an environment where there are multiple people touching the same thing at the same time.' At one point, Craig walked me through all the steps involved in, say, getting a character's hand gesture into the game. First, you see if you can do it yourself, hack something in, get someone to look at it and tell you that, nope, it's not good enough. Then you need to find and hire someone who you think can do it better – which can take months, if not longer. Once you have them, you need to clearly articulate the task and get it into whatever cloud-based tool you happen to be using that week: 'itemize the specific thing, decide on the filename, create the Asana subtask, get it in the spreadsheet over here.' The task needs to be 'teed up': 'maybe I need to capture footage, create a mockup, annotate the mockup, get that all stitched together.' Let's say the gesture then gets made, and you've got the mental bandwidth to have *noticed* it's finished. You then need to meet with Patrick, Sam, and the contributor to review the gesture. Then you ask Patrick to implement it, then you try to figure out how to actually *see* it in order to make sure it's working properly, and, finally, decide if it's good enough, if it's what you wanted, if the gap between expectation and reality is great enough to warrant the hassle of returning to one of the previous steps.

And this is just one of innumerable similar threads active at a given moment. As the ramp-up ramped up, as more and more contributors and vendors were brought on, everything grew more complex. It wasn't just finding voice actors, for example, it was also working with their unions, and – because the onset of this big final push coincided with the start of a global pandemic – doing everything within COVID-19 guidelines: mailing microphones, making sure the actors knew how to use them, making sure they were disinfected before heading to the next address. Craig remembers sitting in on one meeting with a professional voice actor, two people from their audio vendor, A Shell in the

Pit, and Priscilla Snow, whom they had hired to invent the language spoken by the game's characters. 'I'm suddenly in the middle of a legitimate, professional videogame production,' he realized, 'and I'm learning on the job how to make it seem like … or how to *become* an effective director at all of these kinds of things that I'm just learning piece by piece.'

There was a lot to learn – and only so much that *could* be learned, only so much that Craig could do. In retrospect, the central problem was that they kept bringing in more and more contributors, but they didn't hire additional people to manage them. Much of the additional management responsibility landed on Craig, who at some point realized he was doing 'nineteen jobs.' 'I was the owner, I was the biz dev, I was the marketing producer, marketing director, trailer producer, footage capturer – and that's just one department!' He was also playing the triple role of producer, director, and implementer in several other departments: lighting, visual effects, sound effects, writing, environment art, and more. Normally the workflow for a task like the above-mentioned character gesture would go something like this: the Senior Director for JETT contacts the Director of the Character Department, asking them to work with the Character Producer to come up with the Asana tasks for contributors and then monitor how work is progressing; finally, the Character Director gets the material in place for the Creative Director to review. 'But all of those people are me,' Craig realized. 'I'm okay at some of the jobs, even though I'm self-taught. But I'm not good at all of them at once.'

Craig was not the only busy person on JETT. All three of the leads were under enormous pressure through the winter and spring of 2020. Craig described Patrick at this time as, 'like Atlas, holding up the world, making miracles happen on the technical side and being very effective.' Randy Smith was the only person on the project whose remit focused specifically on production. Randy also had nineteen jobs. This was in addition to his game-design duties. It was around this time that Craig realized, 'Even though

Randy is the one person on earth who is absolutely best suited for every part of this project, he's not in and of himself a miracle.'

When I spoke to the JETT team in the summer of 2021, I asked them whether they thought this multiplication of roles and 'amount of overwhelm' (a term they all used) was endemic to videogame productions in general, or to indie games in particular. They held different opinions. Working on his first videogame after many years in TV and film, art director Sam Bradley was immediately struck by the way, on JETT, 'a few people wore a lot of hats.' 'Craig, especially,' he said, 'is a jack of all trades. In terms of the creative process of JETT, he's really hands-on with every single component.' Sam later came to see this as a symptom of the relative immaturity of the game industry. 'Games are still in their infancy,' he told me.

> Maybe they're not babies anymore, but they're still awkward teens at this point. I think there are lots of industry-wide problems that are still a struggle for all people making games. There's a lot of reinventing the wheel from project to project. There's a lot of complexity where other industries have figured out how to unify and streamline and commodify parts of the process in a way that takes some of the weight off of people so that they can focus on the design and creative aspect of it. In games, there's just a lot of weight that hasn't been relieved.

Andy's view was similar. Like Sam, his background was also in film and TV but he had worked on over ten games in the period since he began collaborating on JETT in 2013. What struck him was the sheer amount of 'building up and tearing down' that went on in games. In TV and film, the progress is mostly linear: you build the sets, shoot the scenes, then edit them. Videogames, though, are 'just a blender.' At any point in the project, you can go back in and change something – but everything is so interconnected that changing one part might break three others. As such, 'We're doing final stuff, but we're also rebuilding the sets, so we can't shoot for two months, because there's no sets.'

Speaking with Sam and Andy, I thought of what Virginia Woolf said about female novelists in the modernist period. The novel was the only art form flexible enough to accommodate their urge for experimentation: at a time when 'all the older forms of literature were hardened and set in place,' 'the novel alone was young enough to be soft in her hands.' But because it was so soft and so new, because there were so few rules in place dictating what a novel was or how to write one, writers would get bogged down in figuring all this out, spend a lot of their time fumbling in the dark. 'We must reflect that where so much strength is spent on finding a way of telling the truth,' Woolf wrote, 'the truth itself is bound to reach us in rather an exhausted and chaotic condition.' She concluded, 'We must reconcile ourselves to a season of failures and fragments.'

Randy offered a different account. Back in the sixties and seventies, when games were truly new, people were flying by the seat of their pants. But now, he told me, the steps are known. 'There's been fifty years of refining how to make games without going crazy, breaking the budget, spending too long.' Whereas Andy viewed the everything-at-once 'blender' of JETT production as par for the videogame course, Randy saw it as a 'dirty trap' to be avoided at all costs. The fact that games are, at a technical level, endlessly editable – 'I'll just delete this character, change this tone, add this whole other level' – creates 'this illusion that you have infinite time or infinite resources.' 'But the hard lesson,' Randy said, is that 'every moment you're not going straight for your goal is a resource you've now spent that you'll wish you had at the end of the project.' This was, Randy said, sometimes a hard lesson for JETT's leads. Craig, he said, approached game development the same way he would a commission for a magazine illustration. More specifically, he approached game production like an expert user of software like Adobe Illustrator. It was a matter of, '"I don't love that shape, I'm just going to make it a little bigger." So he's almost done but now he's going to kind of rewind to the beginning.' If this iterative, Ctrl-Z way of working is intuitive to you, Randy said, shifting into videogame production means 'you need to work in very counterintuitive ways if you want to get things done on time.' When I asked Randy to describe his main contributions to the project, he gave the following example: if it seemed like Craig was spending too much time 'trying to get the tree height absolutely correct,' Randy would say, 'No, the tree height is pretty close – say yes, go forward!'

Craig's view of the process was somewhere in between Andy's blender and Randy's known steps. 'It is true,' Craig told me, 'that we had a very hard time calling things finished or fine, and it is true that there were tunings happening throughout.' But all the way through, the project was moving forward, 'purposefully, if experimentally.' 'If two people had made *2001: A Space Odyssey*,' he said, 'learning the relevant crafts of filmmaking and writing along the way, it would have taken time.' The paths of videogame production are inevitably tortuous, in his view – especially 'when a videogame is innovative, risky, exploring some new space, overly scoped or ambitious, and/or driven by relatively inexperienced leads.' Though all those terms applied to him and Patrick, Craig didn't see the game's development in terms of 'a lot of dramatic tearing things down; I see a vast surface area on many layers and two people constructing it piece by piece.'

Such was JETT's path as it approached the PlayStation 5 announce event in the summer of 2020. The event itself, everyone agrees, was a highlight of the project, a thrill and a delight. Everyone got together on Google Hangouts to watch. Sam remembers it as the only time there were too many people on a call to fit everyone's tile on a single screen. For him, it was 'the most exciting team-wide moment.' When the JETT clip played, Craig, Jori, and their two children jumped around in the kitchen for a few minutes. Craig had inserted the Superbrothers logo halfway through the clip, accompanied by the space-baby chime sound, 'calculated to activate all the *Sworcery* heads out there.' He spent that night scrolling through Twitter, enjoying people's reactions: someone, triggered by the sound, had an involuntary muscle spasm and fell off their chair. Still, as Craig told me a month later, 'it's not as if our announce clip set the world on fire.' Yes, ten million people were watching – but JETT was just one of twenty-four games, and 'even among the smaller projects, ours was probably the hardest one to get a grip on.' Craig had a few regrets. It was a shame the pandemic prevented this from being an in-person event: he would have loved to spend time with the team IRL, and to see some of his industry friends in the flesh. More pressingly, it had always been the plan to announce only *after* the game had actually been finished, so that Craig could focus all his energies on marketing. That definitely was not the case here. Instead, the game was slated to ship in less than six months – and, as with *Sworcery*, so much time had been put into crafting the announce clip that progress on the game itself had stalled. When we spoke in late December 2020, by which point the expected launch date had already been missed, Craig wondered if it had been a mistake to put all that energy into the launch clip. 'That's a big question,' he said. 'I'd love to know the answer.'

Summer 2020: in the world of JETT, the best of times, the worst of times. The clip was out, seen by millions. The game was real. But development wasn't on track. With the team fully ramped up, they were burning through as much as $250,000 per month. It was, Craig said, 'bonkers': 'You go through four months of that and, whew: that was' – cue the Dr. Evil voice – '*one million dollars.*' Focused on production of the clip on top of all his other roles, Craig was missing his deadlines. 'People are left hanging, or they don't get the information, or it wasn't quite the right information. There were tasks that were on me to complete in order for us to meet our schedule, and I was not getting them done on time.' And there was always another task to do. Realizing at the last minute that no one had set up the contact email in the announce clip, info@jett.xyz, for instance, he figured that fell under the mandate of one of his nineteen job titles and did it himself.

When we spoke in July of that year, I was full of questions about when exactly in 'Holiday 2020' the game would come out. I needed to know because I needed to get the last chapters of this book written, and I hadn't played the game in over five years. But Craig didn't seem to know. The deadline was 'another thing that I have the heebie jeebies about for sure,' he told me. But 'in part because things have been so hectic,' he said, 'I just don't have the strongest sense of where we are.' He thought Randy probably knew better. 'Because this is kind of my first at-bat with a project remotely like this,' he told me, 'I just don't know how this phase goes. So for a lot of these kinds of concerns – having visibility over the broad project and having conviction about the schedule and things like that – that's kind of the role, one of the roles, that Randy had intended to be playing and is playing to the degree that he can.'

The baseball analogy is as follows: there was a shallow pop fly, everyone thought the other person was going to catch it, and no one called the ball. In later conversations, both Craig and Patrick told me that they were hearing alarm bells at this point. By July 2020, Craig said, 'the writing was on the wall'; they would not ship that calendar year. Both expected Randy, as the most experienced member of the team, to be the one to say, 'Hey, we're in trouble.' Randy, meanwhile, expected the co-owners to make that call. It was not only a case of ambiguous job descriptions, Craig later recalled – it was more evidence that all three of them were overburdened and needed support. The airplane analogy is as follows – this time from Craig:

> It's just, like, we've been trapped on this plane, with our families, for what feels like our whole life. The thought was, okay, let's get some co-pilots in here, see if that helps. Then, when it seemed as if we might miss our runway … I kind of reached over, grabbed the flight stick, and forcibly nosed 'er down.

In summer 2020, Craig and Patrick realized that, as owners of JETT, they needed to take full ownership of its direction. From that point on, they were steering the ship. 'It was not a fun moment,' Craig added, but 'from then on there was credible evidence of a finishing mindset.'

When I spoke to Craig in July 2020, he was in the midst of all this, and just beginning to contemplate the emotional toll that missing the deadline might have on him. 'After so long on this project,' he told me, 'I have needed to believe in a horizon. And so, if that horizon were to shift … I've been trying to find ways not to be psychologically flattened.' 'This project is my entire thirties at this point, pouring hours into it, taking that time from life and family,' he said. 'I've put so much of myself into it, so one does worry about the outcome.' But he needed to learn how to 'put a maximum limit on how much those concerns impact my wellbeing.' He was 'trying to build a compartment where these anxieties can live.'

What dawned on Craig during the summer of 2020, as he put it to me later, was that 'I'm vulnerable, so this project is vulnerable.' Two things needed to be done. First, they needed to get in touch with Sony and officially secure a delay. Second, they needed to bring in additional production support, to relieve Craig of the weight of some of those nineteen jobs. The battle-tested industry veterans they turned to were … Craig's siblings.

Craig's family – his brother Mack and his sister Sarah – proved essential to getting both of these things done, which in turn proved essential to actually, finally finishing the game. JETT, in its finished state, is very much a family affair: if the Adams siblings hadn't come together the way they did, it's very possible that it would not exist at all. No one expected the story of JETT's development to end this way. As Sarah told me, 'The fact that we all joined together is hands-down hilarious.'

Craig described Mack to me as 'The Business Guy,' not just in terms of his role, but also his aura. (For his part, Mack described Craig's entire experience of ramping up production as 'expensive business school.') He was the only person I met with who wore a button-down shirt during our interview. True to his name, Mack is solidly built, with a gruff voice and a no-nonsense demeanor. Still, if he's The Business Guy, it's definitely the West Coast version. His gruff voice is full of wit and memorable turns of phrase; though we spoke for only an hour, I made pages of notes, so quotable were his takes. When he introduced himself to me in an email, he included two links: one to the consulting firm he's been running since 2011, and the other to his photography website. The latter featured albums with labels like 'Grizzly Adams' – *Ursus arctos horriblis* photographed at terrifying proximity – and 'Eastern Bloc & White' – gloomy Iron Curtain apartment buildings in monochrome.

Mack is three years older than Craig and they were close as kids, bonding over videogames in particular (*Teenage Mutant Ninja Turtles* for NES was a favourite). They were renters rather than buyers, frantically trying to get to game's end before it needed to be returned. Mack was involved with Superbrothers from the start – the Super-*brothers* were actually Craig and him – but always in a background role. He advised, he provided support; when I signed my NDA in 2013 I sent it to him. His role expanded during the platform deal period, hiring lawyers, reviewing deals, weighing in with his business advice. But his involvement hit a new level in the summer of 2020, when he recognized that his brother's project – and his brother – needed some help. 'It was just too much,' he told me. 'The machete was just going all day, and no idea if they were going in the right direction.' He told himself, 'Okay, I'm going to wade into the deep end of this.' He was on the call with Sony when they asked for the extension; Craig told me he needed him there for the 'different tone and temperament' he provided, that the gravity of the situation demanded Mack's Business Guy gravitas. The conversation went well: as Craig told me, 'We were met with full understanding and warmth.' The next task was to hire production support. Mack knew the perfect person.

Describing Sarah to me, Craig paused, took a deep breath, and said, 'She's legendary.' Vague, but when I met her I could see what he meant. She has a huge personality: frantically energetic, abounding in effusive hand gestures, owner of a massive laugh. (As with Mack, I wish I could use *all* the amazing material she provided; the Adams siblings, every last one of them, have a way with words.)

Her appearance matched her personality: muscular in a pink Roots hoodie, dog tag necklace, hair close-clipped on the sides. She introduced herself by sending me her CV, which showed vast experience in a vast assortment of fields: undergrad in geography, MBA from McGill, most of a PhD on 'Future-focused decision-making for climate change adaptation' at the University of Queensland in Australia, senior researcher for Tourism British Columbia, Team Leader for a survey of 250,000 BC government employees for Stats BC, Acting Manager for a $1.8M consulting project in the BC public service … and, most recently, Product Marketing Manager for Helm Operations in Victoria – a producer, as Craig put it to me, of 'tugboat software.' Six years older than Craig, she was already off doing all this while he was still in high school. Given the age gap, she wasn't close to Craig the way that Mack was, and they definitely didn't have TMNT or the NES in common. Her main memory of her little brother is playing Lego and He-Man with him to help get him over his bad moods.

The common thread across her diverse CV is her skill as an organizer, irrespective of what she is organizing. The big lesson of her career, as she put it to me, is, 'If you want to do big things, you need people' – and that, as such, however much it runs counter to your inclinations, 'you'll have to accept supervising.' It was a lesson she had resisted, struggled with, and finally learned to embrace. It was exactly what was needed on JETT.

She had no previous experience of any kind in videogames, but that didn't bother anyone. As Mack put it, 'She manages the Amazon boxes, but not what's inside the boxes.' As she put it, 'I have learned that my favourite place to be is completely out of my depth.' It so happened that in late summer 2020, Sarah's involvement in the field of tugboat software was reaching its natural conclusion.

Talking to Mack one day, she said, 'I'm not sure what I'm going to do next.' He said, 'I've got something for you!'

Sarah joined the JETT team in September 2020. Her job, as Craig explained it to me a few months later, 'was to be a mid-level producer more or less assigned to making sense of my world.' No small task. The early months, both agree, were tough. Craig remembers a tortuous onboarding process: explaining not only how this particular game was being made, but, since Sarah was totally new to the industry, how games in general get made. Sarah recalls the emotional state Craig was in at that period, 'We would spend two hours on the phone and he would give me all his fears.' At first, she wasn't sure she was equal to the task before her:

> He was asking me to solve an impossible task, because of the fact that he had nineteen jobs and he was only one person. There was no spreadsheet, no timeline, no thing I could build that would make his life suck less given his approach to doing the nineteen jobs, which was to do them all.

Once she was up to speed, had a sense of the organizational structure and the state of the various operations, she focused on helping Craig communicate effectively to the team. Once, she told him, 'You might as well have dropped this at the bottom of the ocean,' a phrase he quickly picked up on. 'Well, I don't want it to end up at the bottom of the ocean,' he would say. 'Yeah, the bottom of the ocean is a bad place for things!' Craig and Sarah both recalled an early breakthrough: a meeting, led by Sarah, where Craig said only five words, 'Make it 5 percent bluer.' For Sarah, it was evidence that Craig was learning to formulate actionable requests – when she was hired on the project, she implemented a rule: 'Give me a verb and a modifier!' For Craig, it was evidence of the new production pipeline kicking in: the only hat he needed to wear was that of Creative Director, not the other eighteen – to issue imperatives, not execute them.

By the fall of 2020, they had made another key hire in Technical Producer David Rusak, and the gears were starting to turn. Just then, Craig started to feel seriously burned out. 'After all this, *this* is when I get burnout?'

In October, he decided he needed to go into 'quiet time,' strictly limiting his contact time. The idea was to relax and recharge – but he also did a lot of reflecting. 'Boy,' he said to himself, 'I could be a lot better at my job.' Growing up, Craig's father had 'a whole bookshelf of cheesy self-help business books.' During 'quiet time,' Craig became intimately acquainted with the genre. When I spoke to him in December 2020, he was preaching the gospel of David Allen's *Getting Things Done*. 'I would almost consider becoming some sort of evangelist for it,' he said. Reading it was a 'before and after' moment for him – so much so that he actually drew a line on his calendar. As he told me, 'October 17th was the moment when I was able to seize control of my life and my studio space and just lift the fog of my anxiety.' Allen's system is centred on note-taking: its core belief is that we can only think about so many things at one time, and the best way of clearing extraneous tasks from our minds is to write them down. Craig had taken this so much to heart that he had also begun posting self-penned inspirational mottoes around his studio. 'Lift the Fog' was one of them: if you're not organized and haven't planned, you can't see what you're supposed to be working on. ('You have to prepare to die,' he elaborated: 'you have to grapple with that and work backwards.') 'Close Tabs in Mind' was another, something taken from the *Reply All* podcast, but nonetheless 'deeply profound.' Finally, 'Make Life Magic': have energy for the weekend, for the kids, don't just take them for a walk, do something really special. (His example was a haunted house he had put together for his kids with an old tent and some string lights.)

In the months that followed, production achieved a momentum that would continue right through to the end. Craig returned to full-time work after American Thanksgiving, and when he entered the first meeting that Monday morning, he found that no one was expecting him to lead it. Sarah had taken over that duty. 'That was the moment,' he recalled. There was a lot of work ahead, including some brutal 'alpha blocks,' in which they got the scalpel out and performed surgery on certain crucial slices of the game, hoping against hope that doing so wouldn't screw up all the other pieces. But the infrastructure was now in place to get it done. 'Things got ridiculously smoother from March' of 2021, Mack said.

By August 2021, when the game was finally done, Mack reflected, 'Part of the design of this project was this very low-key, low-pressure approach. Low-cost life design. No pressure. No deadlines.' Craig was 'very much trying to avoid the end-of-*Sworcery* style of experience.' And yet, he said, 'we still end up there.' I told him that when I'd spoken to Craig a few days before, he'd said that although it had been tough – that was the day Craig told me, 'I've been in hell for a lot of this' – it was not as tough as *Sworcery*. He had his family, he was in the woods, he had some distance and lots of support. When I told Patrick about Craig's take, he was glad, but surprised: he couldn't imagine anything more stressful than this, but then he hadn't been around for *Sworcery*. Mack, though, said that that sounded about right. 'There's a little less chain-smoking going on.' (The point was metaphorical, for Craig is a nonsmoker.)

A tortuous path, and much structural dread.

And so the question must be asked: Was all this due to the money they took from those two industry behemoths? Ought they to have refused the seven-figures that the platforms offered? Should they have stayed indie and done it themselves?

The best perspective I got on this came from Andy Rohrmann, the member of the JETT Squad with the strongest connections to the historical DIY art community. Andy is polite, affable, and mild-mannered. Sensibly dressed in a plaid shirt, middle-aged, bearded, with a receding hairline, he looks more like an accountant than a member of the avant-garde. But Craig told me that he had stories, and indeed he did. Coming of age in the Seattle/Olympia scene of the 1990s, Andy was not only an observer of the art movement that influenced me more than any other – he was in it.

Andy was a teenager in Seattle in 1991, ground zero in The Year Punk Broke. He was there at the International Pop Underground Convention, the Woodstock of DIY. Co-organized by Calvin Johnson – lead singer of my favourite band of all time, Beat Happening, and co-founder of my favourite label of all time, K Records (whose shield logo another fan, Kurt Cobain, tattooed on his forearm) – the IPU distributed flyers that announced, 'As the corporate ogre expands it's [sic] creeping influence on the minds of industrialized youth, the time has come for the International Rockers of the World to convene in celebration of our grand independence.' The IPU opened with Girl Night, a pivotal moment in the birth of riot grrrl, featuring performances by Bikini Kill and Bratmobile, and the debut of Heavens to Betsy. (The Kill Rock Stars label put out its first record to coincide with the event; without the IPU, *Gone Home* would not have its soundtrack.) Andy was also there when, a month after the IPU, Nirvana released *Nevermind*, and the whole scene exploded. He saw the major label reps at every show, signing all the bands, trying to cash in. He saw the reporters descend, imposing the labels – grunge, alternative, riot grrrl – that helped the record labels sell the records, that reduced Revolution Girl Style Now to a fashion trend.

A few years later, while he was studying industrial design in college, he joined a band of his own, Hush Harbor, and participated in what was left of the idealistic pre-*Nevermind* Seattle/Olympia scene. He played the Yoyo A Go Go festival in 1994, a conscious attempt to recapture some of the magic of the IPU, whose press release defined 'punk rock' as 'a descriptive term that tries to explain the difference between the buy in/sell out culture that wakes us up every morning for work, and the culture so many of us make every day with our own hands.' Hush Harbor appeared on the festival soundtrack alongside Heavens to Betsy, Neutral Milk Hotel, and a barely famous Beck, whose album *One Foot in the Grave* had come out on K Records one month earlier. Later, Hush Harbor recorded for Up Records and became part of the next wave of Seattle-area indie music, sharing roommates and rehearsal spaces with Sunny Day Real Estate and Modest Mouse. When Andy told me this, I explained how important Modest Mouse's *Interstate 8* EP had been to me in high school – that it was maybe *the* record around which I built my identity in those years. 'I did the graphic design for *Interstate 8*,' he told me. I got out my copy, flipped it over to the back, and sure enough: 'design mr. c. a. rohrmann.'

Andy was of the scene, whereas I had merely done my best to absorb it from four thousand kilometres away. Still, I got the sense, talking to him over the years, that he was less attached to it than I was. 'It was great and really formative to be part of that when I was basically a kid,' he told me. 'That's a really cool part of my past that I'm proud of' – but it was part of his *past*, a glorious time that he accepted was over. In the end, Hush Harbor didn't stay together for very long. Andy didn't enjoy the touring life, so he found ways of expressing himself musically that didn't require it, which is how he discovered electronic music and DJing. But music was a hobby in these years: drawing on his education, he made his living in graphic design. Some of this work kept him close to his roots – he did a lot of design for indie record labels – but he was not an ideological purist when it came to selecting clients, not one to make absolute distinctions between 'buy-in/sell-out culture' and DIY art. Indeed, his first paying gig as a musician probably would have horrified his teenaged, IPU-attending, Yoyo A Go Go–playing self. One of his indie-rock graphic design clients got a job with Microsoft – the Corporate Ogre par excellence of the Seattle area – and recommended Andy to do music for a commercial. He got the job, and after that picked up a wide variety of jobs in music: in addition to his work in commercials, TV, and film, Andy produced the only authorized remix of a Bob Dylan song, 'Masters of War,' for the soundtrack to the Ruffian Games/Microsoft Games Studio's title *Crackdown 2*.

As with that first Microsoft gig, Andy's entry into the world of videogames came through the broader indie world. In 2010,

Andy received a message out of the blue from Brandon Boyer, who had published Craig's manifesto 'Less Talk, More Rock' in *Boing Boing* and was then Chairman of the Independent Games Festival. Boyer was a fan of Andy's music and a friend of Craig's, and suggested the two should collaborate on what became the 'Moon Grotto' song for *Sworcery*. Andy was a casual fan of videogames at the time and knew nothing about indie games. He mentioned the prospect of the collaboration to a musician friend of his, Josh Warren, who happened to be obsessed with indie games. Warren's advice was emphatic: 'Do it!' Andy says he likely would have been tempted by *Sworcery* anyway, but it was important to have that 'indie world stamp of approval.' (Warren, whose bands had released albums on K Records and other local indie labels, passed away in 2019. Andy met K Records founder and IPU organizer Calvin Johnson for the first time at his funeral.)

Craig invited Andy to attend GDC in 2012, and Andy was there to see *Sworcery* win the Game Developer Choice Award for Best Handheld/Mobile Game – a massive victory for a tiny game, upsetting industry titans like Nintendo. It was Andy's first time at a big videogame event and his first time hanging out with videogame people. The scene at the GDC brought back memories of the IPU from twenty years earlier – and also of what followed it. He recalled, 'There was a point where I told Craig specifically, "I don't want to jinx anything, but the spirit that's here right now is exactly what I felt in mid-nineties Seattle."' Of course, having actually lived through that period – 'growing up with it, but also being cynical about it' – he perceived this echo in all its ambivalence. He felt the excitement, the sense of doing something genuinely new that people were just starting to pay attention to. But he also sensed the sharks beginning to circle. 'When I was walking around GDC,' he told me, *'everybody* was talking about small games, even the big business people.' The press had also descended, trying to place their labels on the movement. 'You have all these genuine people, but you have just as many hangers-on and people who want to assign a name to it,' he said. 'And it's just this pile-on of people, and then it starts to lose focus.'

'It felt like a bunch of naïve people making cool stuff about to be taken advantage of,' he said. But although he was naturally on the side of the people making the cool stuff, their naïveté – expressed in the same old nineties absolutes of selling out or staying pure, indie versus corporate – was both familiar and frustrating. 'I've noticed this especially with people in the indie community being so antagonistic to anything else,' he told me when we spoke in 2015. 'And it's like, "Well, you're twenty-two and this is your first thing. But when you fall in love and have children, you can't do this anymore. So you might have to go work for one of these companies that you're talking shit about." Which is just reality' – as he knew well himself. In the twenty years since IPU, Andy had learned that he was much more committed to making music full-stop than to attaching himself to particular schools or labels, which he regarded as false anyway – imposed on the scene from the outside, baggage carried in by hangers-on. 'I am old enough and cynical enough to just not give a shit,' Andy told me, and he felt that Craig and he were aligned on this point. As he put it to me in 2015, 'It's amazing and great that there's this indie community – this indie-game scene that's blown up – but neither one of us need it to give us our identity.'

When we spoke again in 2021, I asked him if his perspective had changed, now that the 'peak indie' moment he witnessed at GDC 2012 had run its course. Had the naïve people making cool stuff been taken advantage of? Had the corporate interests and the journalists won? No, he said: things had played out very differently post-GDC as opposed to post-IPU. It was largely because of how different the process of making a game is compared with that of making a record. In the nineties, the major labels had come into Seattle and said, 'Don't worry about anything, just make music, we'll take care of everything else' – record the music, mix and master it, manufacture it, manage the royalties and legalities, promote it, get it into stores. As Andy put it, 'They put bands in a cradle and kept them naïve on purpose,' because it was easier to exploit them that way. With videogames, this just wasn't possible, because you can't make a videogame from a position of naïveté. To make a videogame, you need to know how to operate the machines. 'You're on the floor doing everything,' as Andy said: you're not just the ones writing and performing the music, you're also turning the dials, organizing the schedules, managing the payroll. 'You can be a band and never be a business,' Andy said, 'but it's very, very difficult to make videogames and not face the business end of things.' In music, you're the product, and the label has the control over how it's made. In videogames, you *make* the product, so you have most of the control. All a platform can really say is, 'We'll fund you making this thing for us.' You take the money, and you use it to make the thing you want to make.

From his perspective, they played that role perfectly with JETT, or as well as anyone could. They found the money they needed to make the thing they wanted to make. They took the money and they made the game. At the end of our conversation in August of 2021, I asked Andy, 'All in all, then, not a badly managed project?' 'No!' he replied. 'That's the thing.' The process worked. Those first years, working on their own, with their own money, with no pressure from elsewhere, with only a few contributors here and there, were essential to making the game they wanted to make. 'It's not like after five years we were like, "Whoops, we fucked up and made the wrong game." It was definitely longer than anyone expected. But so much of that was this R&D sculpting, with the eventual idea that it was a videogame. I found all that stuff very valuable.' I asked him about Randy's comment that Craig approached videogame production like an Illustrator user, always reaching for the Undo command. Andy regarded this as a positive, 'a habit that was developed with the freedom not to have to depend on investors or a board of directors' – a 'freedom to experiment that carried on longer than for any company I've been involved with,' and an essential ingredient for making the game they ended up making. As for taking the money from Sony and Epic, that was equally essential. 'This shit is hard,' as he put it. 'It's a lot easier to finish a record than to finish a game, or just quit.' Yes, it's a miracle to make a videogame that corresponds to your vision – but, given the baffling complexity of their construction, it is a miracle just to make a videogame at all. As Andy saw it, they had accomplished both.

In one of our conversations on a different subject – we were talking about the problem of work/life balance and burnout in the games industry – Andy stopped for a second, his eyes scanning the room on his side of the Skype connection as he gathered himself. Then, eyebrows raised, spacing out every word to the length of a sentence, he said, '*I. Cannot. Stop. Making. Music.*' He settled himself and continued. 'My habits, I would say, aren't healthy for most people. When I talk to people who say, "Oh, you just make music and then you're done"' – his eyes scanned the room again – '*I. Don't. Understand. That.* Vacation from work for me is just working on a different thing.' This was the working artist's perspective – the perspective of the ones who stick with it, who keep making art beyond the age of twenty-two. It was also the perspective of Craig and Patrick. They wanted four things, all related. First, to feed their families. Second, to feed their compulsion for making stuff. Third, to make the stuff that they wanted to make. Fourth, for the stuff they made to be good. This quadruple imperative was to be distinguished from the journalist's imperative – *my* imperative, as Andy repeatedly implied in the politest manner possible – which was to place neat labels on the stuff that artists made, to build an efficient filing cabinet for their productions. It was also to be distinguished from the fan's imperative – also mine, as Andy also politely implied – which was all about identity, about building a community for yourself, finding out who you are by finding other people who like the same stuff as you. Andy didn't care about labels and he didn't need a fan community to tell him who he was. The interesting question, from the artist's perspective was not 'Is it indie?' but 'Is it good?'

The question was at the front of my mind when I finally got a beta copy of JETT: *The Far Shore* in the late summer of 2021.

PART IV

SCAN THE HORIZON

10.

I never did become a gamer.

Part of the appeal of this project was the prospect of a journey into the unknown, a trip into an unfamiliar art form, distant cousin to all the stuff I'd spent my life obsessing over. Even when I thought it would take only a couple of years to finish, I figured if you signed up to write a book about a videogame, you'd inevitably come out on the other side as an initiate. It was hard to imagine, but maybe I'd become one of those people who pontificate about *BioShock* and stay up into the early hours playing *Call of Duty*. Maybe I'd buy one of those complicated, loud-coloured chairs designed just for gaming, the ones that look like they've been ripped out of a race car.

Games did become part of my life. I played a bunch of games, mostly indie. I published academic articles about games. I taught games in my classes. I even learned how to make simple games in Twine and put together a series of Twine tutorials on YouTube that became fairly popular. But I never became a gamer.

Not that I didn't try. In 2017, I even bought a console. Some of my students had started a videogame study group that met weekly at cafes around town, and I would join them at Ezra's Pound or Red Rocket Coffee to listen in on their heated debates about interactivity and *Fortnite* and eSports. They were all convinced that, as an old person who was curious about this art form of theirs and looking to go deeper, I would like Nintendo's new Switch platform: it had great specs, you could play it at home or on the subway, and it also had a bunch of games that were specially designed to target middle-aged nostalgia. When I talked to Craig that year, he agreed: the Switch and its most famous nostalgia triggers, *Zelda: Breath of the Wild* and *Super Mario: Odyssey*, were not to be missed.

(He was particularly obsessed with *Breath of the Wild*, and would use it as a reference point in his Silicon Valley slideshow in 2019.) Around this same time, I got a text from a friend who knew I was writing this book and who insisted I play *Breath*. I asked him what was so great about it and he explained that he'd just tamed a horse and was currently riding it around a landscape evoking medieval Japan. I placed my order.

For the first couple of months, it worked. I loved how designed and purposeful the worlds felt. Everything was there for a reason: if there was a piece of fabric on the ground, it was so that you could use it as a kite; if a tower could be climbed, it was so that you could use your kite to hang-glide off to another land. It struck me that this was what it must be like to really believe in God. The whole environment was a feedback system: everything could be interpreted as a sign of divine favour or displeasure. It was the world of William Bradford, whose journal *Of Plymouth Plantation* I'd read in my Intro to American Lit class. Crossing the Atlantic in the Mayflower, Bradford had interpreted every storm to mean someone onboard had sinned, every ray of sunlight as a sign the pilgrims were on the right path. I found myself looking for omens in the real world, too, searching for meanings in a full moon or branch swaying in the breeze. I started to understand Craig's experience after playing *Zelda: Ocarina of Time*, which led him to try living as if the real world were a videogame, as if it were charmed, as if everything he encountered had meaning, bore the mark of a Creator.

But the games were also frustrating. If I got stuck, if I got lost, if I couldn't beat a boss, if the God of this world seemed indifferent to my adventures, I would lose my temper. For the rest of the day, I would walk around tense, like I'd been in an argument. And the games wanted so much of my time. I'd been playing *Breath of the Wild* for ten, twenty hours, and it still felt like I was only beginning; I still hadn't met the horse, much less tamed it. If I spent one of my frustrating evenings with *Odyssey* – mistiming my cannonade for the hundredth time, smashing my controller, yelling at my

TV – later I'd lie awake in bed, adrenaline pumping, wondering why I hadn't just read a book instead.

Eventually, that's what I started doing. I remember the sheer relief of spending a night reading a biography of W. H. Auden: I didn't get mad, I learned some odd new words, and eventually the act of reading put me to sleep. After a few months with Zelda and Mario, I returned the Switch to its case, stuck it in a drawer, and never touched it again. A couple of years later, in the first few months of the pandemic, I read that Nintendo was finding it impossible to keep up with surging demand. Hoping that my Switch might be of use to some stranded soul, I took it out of its drawer and put it up on eBay, where it sold for twice what I'd paid for it.

So when I finally got my copy of JETT, I had nothing to play it on. The Switch wouldn't have done me any good, but I'd never bought a PlayStation, either. All I had were my old Mac – good enough for the indie games I continued to favour, but not much else – and an off-brand PS4 controller I'd bought for my original JETT playtest in 2015. But the game didn't work on Macs; in fact, it needed serious modern hardware to run properly. PS5s were unattainable that summer (another pandemic supply chain casualty), so there was nothing to be done but to buy a PC 'gaming laptop.' I read some reviews online, then headed to Best Buy to pick up the machine that most publications agreed was best: an angular black Asus with a military aesthetic and an absurd quasi-mythical name, Zephyrus. On the back of the screen, pointing out at the world, as if proclaiming something essential about the laptop's user, was a badge that read 'R.O.G.: Republic of Gamers, Est. 2006.'

After leaving Best Buy, I went to an outdoor food court I'd heard good things about, which had just reopened after the latest lockdown. When my waiter – a young and jovial fellow in a patterned short-sleeve button-down shirt and khaki shorts – went to put my glass of water on the table, he spilled it all over my lap, mercifully missing the new laptop. After apologizing for his clumsiness, he explained that it was his first shift in ages, that he hadn't had any human contact in months. With a conspiratorial wink in the direction of my shopping bag, he told me he'd been spending eighteen hours a day on *World of Warcraft*.

'By the way,' he added, 'sweet rog.'

Rog? It was a word I had never encountered before, not even in Auden. Did he have an accent? Did he mean 'rug'? Did he think I was wearing a toupee?

Seeing that I looked puzzled, he clarified by asking about graphics cards: 'Does it have the RTX?'

Right, of course: my laptop. R.O.G. It was a shibboleth, literally, and I didn't know the pronunciation. I may have owned the laptop, but I was no citizen of the Republic of Gamers.

'What's your game?' he asked, giving me one last chance.

I told him I was writing a book about a game called *JETT*, with two Ts.

'Never heard of it,' he said.

It's weird trying to review something that no one else has ever seen – to figure out, all on your own, whether something new is any good.

When I was in my early twenties, I started an online music magazine with some friends. I did this mostly for the review copies, which were free and which you got months before the release date. But then you had to say something about them. With no one else's opinions to provide balance, mine were wildly exaggerated: everything felt like either a masterpiece or a piece of trash. Inevitably, after a few months or years had passed, I'd listen to a record I'd initially rated as 100 percent, find it was just okay, and go back and edit the review. Eventually, I decided it wasn't worth the free CDs, and so the venture ended.

Virginia Woolf talks about this problem in 'How It Strikes a Contemporary' – one of my favourite of her essays because it finds her asking such a vulnerable question, a question that feels impossibly touching from our own perspective, where she's recognized as probably the greatest English-language writer of the twentieth century: Is my work any good? Every writer, as she puts it, 'has a natural desire to know whether his [*sic*] own work, produced with infinite pains and in almost utter darkness, is likely to burn for ever among the fixed luminaries of English letters or, on the contrary, to put out the fire.' It's a problem not only for writers, who want to know whether they're wasting their time, but also for what she calls 'the great republic of readers' ('By the way, sweet ror'), who want to know whether theirs is being wasted. Reviewers are useless to both:

> Two critics at the same table at the same moment will pronounce completely different opinions about the same book. Here, on the right, it is declared a masterpiece of English prose; on the left, simultaneously, a mere mass of wastepaper which, if the fire could survive it, should be thrown upon the flames.

They're aligned on the classics: 'both critics are in agreement about Milton and Keats,' who obviously 'display an exquisite sensibility and have undoubtedly a genuine enthusiasm.' But when it comes to their contemporaries, they're all over the place. New books, Woolf says, are the ones we need most: 'Every day we find ourselves doing, saying, or thinking things that would have been impossible to our fathers,' and 'New books lure us to read them partly in the hope that they will reflect this re-arrangement of our attitude.' But show the same book to two critics and see it declared 'at once a lasting contribution to English literature and a mere farrago of pretentious mediocrity.' Woolf ends her essay with advice for people in my situation: follow the example of 'that gaunt aristocrat, Lady Hester Stanhope, who kept a milk-white horse in her stable in readiness for the Messiah and was for ever scanning the mountain tops, impatiently but with confidence, for signs of his approach.'

'Scan the horizon,' Woolf counsels, 'and so prepare the way for masterpieces to come.'

Inevitably, when I first played JETT, my responses were chaotic. I felt like I had both of Woolf's critics inside my head at once, left side and right side, declaring the game a masterpiece one second, wastepaper the next.

My very first impression was dismal. Once I finally got my ROG set up, once the beta build's many gigabytes had been transferred from the Google Drive servers onto my new hard drive, the first thing I heard sounded like a bad joke. An inscrutable symbol appeared on the screen, and then a rough, wavering voice started speaking to me in a language I didn't understand. 'A people reborn in Ghoke's dim glow,' the subtitle said, with stilted diction that was hard, grand, out of date – the tone of epic, of Milton's *Paradise Lost*: 'Arise … outpace oblivion … be resolute.' 'Old craggly voice,' I wrote in my notes. 'Cheesy sci-fi wizard.' The voice emitted a long, contemplative grunt that was all too familiar. It was trisyllabic, an amphibrach, unstressed-stressed-unstressed: *mmmMMMmmm*. 'Oh god,' I noted, 'the wizard just grunted like Yoda.'

But then I pressed the space bar and awoke into a gorgeously mysterious scene. The air was filled with suspended spores; walking through them felt like traversing the night sky. Strange figures in straw hats encircled a woman with an impressive braid identified as 'Synth Mystic,' owner of the craggly voice. They referred to me as Mei and invited me to look at some old manuscript pages, then the display glitched out into some kind of vision of the future. The mystic told me to leave, and there I was, in the steppe scene from the trailers, a world of intoxicating movement. A milk-white horse rustled impatiently as I exited the yurt. The tall grass swayed, as did a small congregation of well-wishers, who bobbed back and forth in unison like inflatable clowns all punched by the same hand. 'This world looks fucking awesome,' I noted. I spoke to Mei's family, appreciated more details – a *Sworcery*-esque stag's skull on a pike, a weather-beaten winged statue, hot air balloons on the horizon – and followed my co-pilot Isao to our jett. Back in real life, my partner walked by, looked over my shoulder at the screen, told me she loved the pilots' reflection in the windshield of the jett and commented that Mei and Isao, with their shaggy haircuts and Nehru suits, reminded her of the Beatles. I fumbled through the flight training, then found myself genuinely unsettled by Cosmodrome z-13, the launch site: gas fires everywhere, evoking the burning Kuwaiti oil fields of Werner Herzog's *Lessons of Darkness*; banners and barbed wire separating the pilots from the commoners who had come to see them off. Then launch, a thousand years pass, and we've reached the far shore, 'Our new home, if all goes well.' A beautiful parachuting sequence, Tor peeking through the clouds like Mount Fuji, then trying to coax our damaged jett to land. 'This isn't all balls-out madness,' I noted. 'You're weak and vulnerable.' I reached a rocky outcrop, butterflies filled the air, and Isao suggested we mark this momentous occasion – a thousand-year journey, a prophecy fulfilled – by building an inukshuk. An option appeared on my screen: 'E: Undertake devotion.' I wrote in my notes, 'THIS GAME RULES!!'

In its finished form, JETT: *The Far Shore* felt both familiar and deeply strange. I had been seeing it for years, I knew its narrative inside and out – both the story it tells and the story of its creation. But here it was at last, fleshed out in parts, pared down in others – no longer a constellation of possibilities but an actual thing.

Though some names and details had changed, the contours were the same. After pilot training in the Prologue, after the thousand-year journey to the far shore and the landfall sequence, in Act I, you set about exploring the planet and learning how to fly your jett. To power your ship's scramjets, you need something called vapour, and, conveniently, it's all over the landscape. You look for colourful patterns on your ship's 'resonator' to find a place to shelter. You meet the local flora and fauna, deer-like figures named hoppas who get freaked out when you pop your jett too close by, flowerlike clusters called ghokebloom that love getting popped – they seem to come to life, then send you flying blissfully into the air.

In Act II, you help establish Ground Control, your home base on the planet. In the process, you meet some more local wildlife, including an incomprehensibly massive creature floating in the sky. He's called a kolos – a name applied to any large creature on the planet – and he doesn't seem thrilled to have you here. But you manage to distract him and complete your task. Once Ground Control is established, you get to know the rest of the crew. Misha, the leader, and Pasha, the chief medic, are wise and patient. Jones, the commander of the scouts, is cynical and daring; Caro, her co-pilot, has a piercing stare and an asymmetrical haircut. Wu, a botanist, is sweet and full of wonder. Her co-pilot Vic, also an engineer, is an interstellar Ron Swanson, moustachioed and gruff.

Act III begins with a long sequence in Ground Control in which you learn the details of your mission. You're here to gather scientific observations about the planet to transmit for analysis to the Mother Structure – the ship in which you travelled for those thousand years, currently in orbit. Your first task is to track the source of the hymnwave, the mysterious radio transmission that beckoned your people here, which seems to be originating from Tor, the huge symmetrical mountain on the horizon. Before setting out, though, you and your crew get together to celebrate the tsoultide (Craig's beloved solstice, thinly disguised) which involves eating soup, reciting passages from Tsosi's tsagas (the Tolstoy figure's prophetic epic), and contemplating your situation. Isao marvels at the correspondence between this world and the world of Tsosi's text, particularly Tor's shape, 'so alike to how it is in the tsagas.' But, ominously, Jones says, 'the tsagas are elsewhere replete with grievous error.' Isao agrees: 'It's those contradictions that are so troubling.' (It doesn't help that *we*, as Mei, are the one everyone expects to resolve these contradictions: as the lone mystic in the group, we've been initiated in Tsosi's lore and have personally experienced the hymnwave, whatever that means.)

On that ambivalent note, it's off to Tor, where players like me – the ones who've come to JETT for the Superbrothers sauce, which is to say the mind-bending and abstract – finally get their reward. Exploring a cleft in the mountainside, you and Jones are caught in a rockslide, your suits are pierced, and you are cut off from your comrades. Then you experience a vision – or that's what it must be, because you seem to be talking to a demonic version of yourself: a Mirror Mei with glowing eyes and a synthesizer voice. 'Time to let slip our masks of innocence,' Mirror Mei says. 'Time to reckon with who we are. Time to relinquish our hegemonic vision.' Then, suddenly, you're somehow back at the start of the game, back at Mei's home in the steppes – although everything is changed, is uncanny, and seems to have been transformed into a shadow of itself. When you try to approach your family, they disappear like ghosts. A stag's head lies burning in front of the yurt, trigons rising like smoke. Inside, you speak to the Yoda-voiced mystic, who is now renamed The Wyld and whom I vaguely understood to be the voice of Tor. She has the same message as Mirror Mei, plus a threat: 'Relinquish your hegemonic vision – abdicate and respire for a while to come. Or do as you do and die, none remaining to mourn. … Tor is kindled, the die is cast,' The Wyld says, obliquely and with menace. 'Now we'll see how far you go.'

With that, you're ejected from the Tor Cleft, escorted by a nasty crew of winged creatures called griefers. As you scramble back to Ground Control, Tor emits something called a dreadwave, which knocks out your communication gear. Afterward, a belligerent Hitchcockian throng settles over Ground Control, rendering it inoperable. The tone of the game from this point on is dark. Whereas Acts I and II are filled with awe, wonder, and hopeful anticipation, Act IV is dominated by angst. Jones, who has also experienced a vision inside Tor, asks you, 'Did we encounter a conscious being? Or were our experiences just psychedelic nonsense?' She is acting strange, and eventually the medic Pasha comes up with an explanation: this planet you've alighted on is somehow alive inside Jones. When her suit was pierced, she inhaled some ghokebloom spores, and the seemingly benign plant has acted as a vector through which her consciousness has been breached. The planet's entire ecosystem is some kind of linked mind – and now Jones is part of it. Since Mei's suit was also pierced, whatever is in Jones is in you too. You've come as colonizers, but now, as Jones notes, 'We've been colonized. The irony is not lost.'

The action of Act IV involves struggling to re-establish the uplink to the Mother Structure. A ground kolos – a creature resembling a rhinoceros – has inadvertently made off with your comms gear, and it's become lodged in his hide. You need to sneak up on him to pry it out – a task that requires patience and ingenuity. You recover the gear, but the uplink doesn't work, and then it's stolen by yet another kolos – an aquatic one, this time, resembling a giant squid. You must travel to an icy island called Khovd – it's pronounced COVID; JETT is thick with prophecy – to get it back, and an uncharacteristically violent encounter with the squid-kolos ensues. The crew's botanist justifies the battle as 'a slaughter, in the cause of survival,' but Isao remains perturbed. 'Our encounter with that ocean kolos – it shook me,' he says. 'This isn't who I thought we'd be.'

Following another, less violent, battle with immaterial creatures called phosfiends, the uplink is finally established, and your findings are at last transmitted. But it is an empty victory. What you have accomplished on the far shore is modest – it may contribute to the eventual aim of building a new home here, but you can't be sure. Indeed, if anything, your quest has made that goal seem less realistic, not more. As Jones puts it, the planet is deeply ambivalent to your presence, 'at odds with itself': 'The wyld, the hymnwave – they beckon to us, ask us to carve out a future here. But Tor itself, the griefers, the throng – all seem opposed.' Jones, increasingly erratic as she comes under the spell of wyld, has gone missing during one of the altercations, and her present whereabouts are unknown. Then Misha, the leader, announces that the entire crew has been contaminated with ghokebloom, you are all in a state of 'synthesis.' The only thing to do, she says, is to return to Ground Control and go back into torpor – to hope that the findings you've managed to transmit might, somehow, some day, be used to devise a cure for your contaminated minds.

The end.

I spent a full week playing through JETT – not quite eighteen hours per day, but close. By the end, *my* mind was contaminated, full of contradictory impressions that needed sorting out. Thankfully, my final big interviews with Craig and Patrick were coming up. Who better to help me work though my feelings about JETT than the people who had made it?

Alas, they were of no help.

One of the things I've discovered in the thousand years since I started writing this book is that I'm a good runner. In 2013, I'd been on a couple of jogs. By 2021, I'd run a bunch of marathons, including Boston, and had discovered a particular talent for middle-distance on the track. In early August 2021, when I finally got to talk to the JETT team about the game they had created, the Olympics were on in Patrick's adoptive hometown, and I was all amped up, getting up every morning at ungodly hours to watch the track races, then pretending I was in Tokyo when I ran in Toronto in the evenings. The night before I spoke to Craig and Patrick, I'd been in an 800m race, and I'd let Olympic fever get the best of me. I ran a brave race, pushing hard through the first lap in sixty seconds, then making a huge move with 200m to go to take the lead. I'd built up a big gap by the home stretch and was on pace to break two minutes – a huge personal best, and a bit of a feat for a forty-year-old. But just as I was approaching the line, I tripped over my own feet and came crashing down face-first onto the track. My head landed on the finish line, but your time depends on when your *shoulder* crosses, and mine was still a few centimetres short. A few people passed me before I was able to roll over the line in 2:04, still a good time, but no 1:59. The next morning my hand, elbow, and knees were covered in bandages. Harder to bandage were the cuts and scrapes on my face. I was about to conduct the most important interviews of this entire book, and I looked like I'd been in a bar brawl.

But again, as always on this project, the embarrassing situation took on symbolic resonances. The two people I spoke to that day seemed to be in the same situation. They'd run a brave race, they had been ambitious and bold, and had pushed themselves absolutely to the limit. They had crossed the finish line, with a result that I came into the interview thinking was impressive. But they both seemed battered.

Going into the interviews, my head full of all those disorganized thoughts about JETT, I only prepared a few questions: 'What part of the game are you proudest of?' and 'What do you think the reception will be?' I really just wanted to know what they thought the cool parts were, so we could geek out about them together.

Time zones being what they are, I spoke to Craig first, and I was floored when he – the most loquacious of interlocutors, someone who only ever spoke in endless streams of perfect paragraphs – had almost nothing to say. What was he proudest of? He couldn't think of anything, because, as he told me, 'To be honest, I can't play it right now.' Mostly, that was because he was too busy fixing bugs and getting ready for launch. 'But even if you were to say, "Here's a whole day where you've got nothing else except time to play the videogame," I think I'd really struggle to progress through it. Because it's just a battlefield for me.' A battlefield: although JETT is a nonviolent game whose landscapes evoke wonder and awe, for Craig it was literally that, a terrain over which every inch was the result of intense creative combat. He couldn't comment on the cool parts. 'Everything that's not quite where I'd like it to be creates the question of, "Okay, but do you just make your peace with it or do you write something down about it or … "' Not only was he incapable of playing the game now, he told me, 'I've got no aspiration to being able to play it some day.' As to the likely reception, 'I hope that what we do hits the target, is in the right spirit, and so, to the degree that people feel good about that, great.' But, he said, 'I don't have too much energy or expectation in that direction.' His voice was weary. 'I'm still pretty depleted.'

The only thing on Craig's mind that day – the only idea he wanted to discuss – was whether it was possible to make a video-game without enduring the hell that he had just been through. 'You're talking to a changed person after the experience of the last couple years,' he said. 'My quality of life from here is paramount … I'm trying to move toward a place where my life resembles something that I would enjoy.' That meant moving away from projects like *JETT*, unless he could discover some totally different way of making games. 'Could there be a structure that exists where I'm not overwhelmed?' he wondered. When I asked about possible next projects, he said, 'Given what I've been though, there is no point in me getting excited about a new creative project.' He added, with that same weariness, 'Unless all these structural issues are resolved, there's no point in getting particularly excited about anything.' The person whose immensity of vision had so amazed me over those three days in the woods of Quebec in 2013 now said, 'The other thing is making sure that any future projects are just *not ambitious*. Channel whatever that ambition is into something of extremely limited scope and complexity.' I wanted Craig's perspective on the game, but he was still too close to the project to have any.

I spoke to Patrick later that day – after the sun had set here and was just rising over Tokyo. More emotionally moderate than Craig, riding the mean to Craig's dips and spikes, I expected a more balanced take. But though his response was calmer and more worked-through, it was identical in substance. Like Craig, he fully recognized his own lack of perspective: as he told me, 'working on a game, you're training yourself to see all the problems with it, so that you can fix them – so there's definitely a bit of tunnel vision.' Pressed to name the things he was proudest of, he managed to generate at least a flash of enthusiasm. 'In a lot of ways, I basically built this whole game,' he said. 'Craig did the level work, but I built all of the tool sets for making that happen, and all of the flight model is basically me, and all of the gameplay mechanics – they got tuned somewhat by other people, but it's basically all … *me*. So I have a lot of pride in general that the game exists, and it's a fairly complex thing.' Despite this pride, though, the dominant feeling for Patrick was of wasted time and effort. 'When I reflect on JETT and my life as a whole,' he said, 'I don't think I can square the effort with the result in a way that is especially positive for my whole-life view. If you think about spending eight years of your life working hard on something, and having it be like a semi-mediocre videogame release … '

I let out an exasperated chuckle when he said that: *semi-mediocre videogame release*. It seemed absurdly pessimistic. In response to my exasperation, Patrick smiled too; maybe he was joking. He took a second to reconsider what he'd just said – and then he stood by it. 'Hopefully it's better than that,' he said, 'but it's not top world-class, I don't think. It's a decent videogame that is fresh or whatever. But it's still a lot of your life to invest into that.' But what if it came out and was a huge hit, and got raves from all the critics – would that change how he felt about it? 'Personally I feel that the game we made is not as good as I would have wanted to make, given that many years of work,' he replied. 'But being stuck to it for so many years, it's hard to have a clear sense. If the general public response is extremely positive or something, I'd have a harder time feeling like that.'

Thankfully I wouldn't need to wait very long for that public response to start flowing in.

You can tell a lot about the health of an art form from its reviewing culture. The two best indicators are quantity of reviews and the likelihood of a roast. I'm not aware of any published reviews of my academic book *Literature in the Digital Age*: quantity zero, bad sign. If you publish a book of poetry in Canada today, you might get a review in a trade publication or, if you're really lucky, a newspaper – and if you do, it's guaranteed to be positive, because the feeling is that trashing a book of poetry is like flogging a dead horse, so imperiled is the genre. So also, in the grand scheme, not a good thing.

But the world of videogames nails both metrics. Reviews abound. When a new game comes out, there is endless talk about it – in magazines both digital and (yes) print, on YouTube, on forums, on Twitter, on Twitch. And everyone, from the fanboys to the professional critics, feels authorized to speak their minds. When *No Man's Sky* and *Cyberpunk 2077* came out and were disastrous, reviewers called them on it. And in both cases, this was all to the good: their developers used this feedback to fix the issues, improve their games, and deliver the classics they'd promised all along.

JETT benefitted from this robust reviewing culture even before it was released. In late August, just over a month before launch, a number of major publications published 'previews' – exactly like a review, with full potential for a takedown, but focused only on a limited section of the game, in this case the Prologue and Acts I and II. It was a limited slice, it didn't contain the scenes I personally found most fascinating, but it was still crucial stuff, and I had high hopes that these reviewers would give me the perspective that Craig and Patrick had so totally lacked – that they would help me to frame the game and settle my thoughts.

There were, at least, some points of consensus in the previews. For instance, everyone said exactly the same two things about the flight model. On the one hand, flying it at speed was awesome. *Pushsquare* said 'piloting the jett' was 'a highlight of the game'; 'it's fun just flitting about.' *Gamereactor* called it 'incredibly satisfying'; PC *Gamer*, 'genuinely thrilling' and 'pretty damn satisfying'; *Eurogamer*, 'an absolute joy.' IGN couldn't stop enthusing on this particular point: jett-piloting was 'a consistent thrill,' 'pure bliss,' 'singularly thrilling,' sheer 'wizardry.' (The only dent in Patrick's justified pride for all this was that IGN attributed it to the wrong wizard: 'Superbrothers has nailed a certain feel to the speed and movement of the jett,' they wrote – but it was *Pine Scented* who had struck that particular nail on the head.) On the other hand, though, when you turned the boosters off and slowed down, the controls were annoyingly fiddly. Reviewers complained about how easy it was to get tangled in a tree or snagged on a rock, how hard it was to make any kind of finessed movement. (These complaints shocked and relieved me: I got tangled in trees all the time, but I thought it was because I sucked at videogames.)

On less technical or immediately visceral matters, though, the reviewers behaved exactly as Woolf predicted. They were hopelessly muddled. One review called the character design 'beautiful and original'; another said JETT's characters had the 'off-putting build of a Playmobil figure.' One reviewer described himself as 'genuinely enraptured by the world(s) the developers are creating'; others were bored. *Gamereactor* was incensed by a sequence in Act I that gives the player some free time: 'I was asked to patrol and research a small set of sandy islands for 20 minutes … needless to say, after around five minutes, I found myself desperate for things to do.' (Twenty minutes of exploring a landscape that had taken its creators eight years to build: perish the thought!) *PC Gamer* warned, 'If you're planning on climbing into this JETT with Mei, you'd better pack a bit of extra patience in the cargo bay': 'When you're not speeding around the planet you'll take a lot of long walks through corridors at your base, sit down for meals, observe cultural rituals, and stand still while everyone else has a good long chat they seem in no hurry to wrap up.' But this slow pace was exactly what *Eurogamer*'s reviewer liked best about JETT. 'It is purposefully slow,' he wrote. 'You'll stop to look at things, your objective might be to just scan local wildlife for 20 minutes.' 'I am all about this,' he said: 'more quiet time please, everyone slow the hell down and actually enjoy the thing you're playing, the space you're occupying.' *Rock Paper Shotgun*'s reviewer was generally befuddled by JETT, but loved the mellow soup-sharing ceremony. 'Might carry that on in real life, to be honest,' he said.

But it's not just that the reviewers disagreed with one another; they seemed to disagree with themselves. They weren't confused; they were ambivalent. This prevailing mood was best expressed by the reviewer for *Gamereactor*. 'There aren't many games that truly leave me uncertain these days,' he wrote. 'Whether a title is remarkable or the polar opposite, I usually have plenty to say about it, but JETT: *The Far Shore* […] has left me pretty bewildered.' He went on to call the game both 'unusual' and 'very unusual.' *PC Gamer's* reviewer was equally disoriented by JETT's peculiar 'mixture of melancholy and hope,' which produced another stutter: 'The alien world is moody and strange and truly feels alien.' The *Rock Paper Shotgun* review opened with the lurid simile 'I downloaded space adventure game JETT: *The Far Shore* like a dog waiting to lick clean a planet' – but it ended up in the same uncertain state: 'I'm still unsure whether this new alien taste in my mouth is one I want to keep eating when it comes out in full on October 5th.'

Most of these reviews presented their ambivalence as temporary, something that would be resolved once they'd had a chance to play the rest of the game. But the most perceptive review, in IGN, suggested that ambivalence was a permanent and essential aspect of JETT. This had to do with its narrative. JETT is about a group of people who have been driven from their home – their planet, their culture, their families – by the imperative of survival. Their quest, as the IGN reviewer noted, is 'enticing yet sad' – both at once. After a thousand years in torpor, everyone they used to know is now dead, their civilization destroyed. 'The mission players are embarking on is the culmination of centuries of work' – and 'there is pressure to that, and certain expectations.' But the world is also beautiful, and the prospect of a future is comforting. 'Seeing how Mei and her fellow explorers grapple with that' – the weight of their task – 'while also appreciating the wonder and the thrills of that actual work, is fascinating to see unfold.'

I went to the JETT previews hoping to come away with some essential insight, something to ground my own understanding of the game, some anchor for my experience. And I got it.

The people who played *JETT* felt ambivalent – because *JETT* was *about* ambivalence. The experience matched the narrative.

That was something to hold on to. I put it in my pocket.

Andy described the process of making *JETT* as 'a blender.' Finishing this book was a bit of a blender, too. I finally got my build in July 2021. In early August, I conducted interviews. Then I had to transcribe the important parts of these interviews, and – finally knowing how the story ended – listen back to all the hours and hours of interviews I'd conducted since 2013, seeking out the bits that hadn't seemed important at the time but that, given how everything turned out, had become essential. Then I wrote the making-of section, which I wrapped up in early September, while at the same time grappling with my thoughts for this section, the one about whether the game was good. Somewhere in there, *JETT*'s release had been announced for October 5th. I wanted to be able to put a short description of the launch into an epilogue, and Coach House wanted the book on shelves for Holiday 2021. That meant that the book needed to be completely finished on October 7th and printed on the 12th. But we hadn't even started editing. So it was a blender. The day the *JETT* previews came out, in addition to reading them I was also transcribing my interview with Sarah and editing the scene where I visit Craig in the woods in Quebec in 2013, which I'd written in 2016. I was in every part of the book at once, it was all in my head. Which was confusing, but gave me another idea about how to evaluate *JETT*.

Editing my way through the manuscript, every time I came across a part where Craig or Patrick explained some goal they hoped to achieve with the game they were making, I noted it in a document I called 'Yardsticks.' This way, I'd be asking something much more concrete and less subjective than 'Did some random dudes who a few random game magazines happened to assign to reviewing *JETT* like the first two hours?' or 'Did *x* part of the game happen to appeal to me, with my peculiar tastes and biases and quirks, and my particular needs as a guy writing a book about that game?' The question would be, 'Did Craig and Patrick make the game they wanted to make?'

Once again, it was tricky.

They wanted to make all dialogue optional, to avoid all cutscenes, to give players full control over how much lore they dug into. Had they achieved all that? No. You could sometimes decide to end a conversation early, but as the PC *Gamer* reviewer said, there were a bunch you couldn't avoid, and those seemed to go on and on. JETT wasn't overflowing in cutscenes, but there were plenty, from the thousand-year journey to the tsoultide ceremony. Not that this was a problem, necessarily; for me and some of the reviewers, those were among the most moving parts of the game. As for lore, there was plenty. Even if you didn't decide to spend hours at the little television screen in Ground Control that I came to call LoreTV (I was a fan of the programming), the hymnwave, the wyld, the tsagas, they were all unavoidable.

Craig and Patrick wanted to have players go off and learn to subsist in an alien ecosystem. Besides the much-lamented twenty minutes after landfall, that wasn't really part of the game. The action was all very much on rails. The scene where Isao allows you to Undertake Devotion and builds an inukshuk is followed by an abrupt transition: one minute he's saying, 'Mei, let's hold this moment close'; the next, he's insisting, 'Only, it's time we attend to our next task.' Someone was always telling you what to do.

They wanted to make narrative reality and gameplay one and the same; they wanted to 'exercise benign thought processes.' They had certainly avoided the trap of squeezing their story into the usual kill-or-be-killed bloodbath. The mechanics were nonviolent, your ship didn't have lasers, you were always doing your best to accomplish your task without harming anyone. In the heart-pounding moments, you were usually running away from something, trying to put it gently to sleep, politely asking it to please, if at all possible, hand something over that belonged to you anyway, if that wasn't too much trouble (it was such a Canadian game!). My favourite mechanic was bolstering ghokebloom:

I never fully understood its purpose beyond expanding my vapour tank capacity, but I had the sense that there was something symbiotic in the gesture, that the planet wanted its ghokebloom bolstered (I loved that verb, 'bolster'), that the ghokebloom had been waiting centuries for me to arrive to do it, that its response to my doing so – sending me flying gently into the air – was an expression of immense pleasure. But there was no Jerk Mode. Although Isao would occasionally scold you for popping too close to a hoppa, remind you to 'tread lightly' or 'avoid stirring up trouble,' there were no great consequences if you ignored him, and the game didn't seem to remember your bad behaviour or punish you for it later.

And the gameplay could still feel arbitrary. The jellyfish-collecting task I'd complained about in the 2015 build was still in the finished game, awkwardly placed after the moment of high tension in which Mei and Jones come to grips with the realization that they've been 'bewyldered' – that their minds are being invaded by the planet. One moment you're talking to Jones about super-organisms and collective intelligence, and the next, Isao is explaining how to build a repair kit by grappling five shinggs.

The issues weren't only with the integration of narrative and gameplay, but also with the narrative itself. Although the macro-narrative of JETT – ecological collapse, a thousand-years' journey, a planet that beckoned us but seems hostile to our arrival – was engrossing and awe-inspiring, the micro-narrative could feel both repetitive and silly. You lose your uplink to the mothership, you re-establish it, but then lose it again, and finally re-establish it once more. Both times, exactly the same thing has happened: a kolos has taken your antenna, and it has become lodged in its hide. As Randy memorably put it, a reasonable plot summary of JETT: The Far Shore might go as follows: 'the kolos stole my cell-phone ... twice.'

So did Craig and Patrick achieve their goals, did JETT measure up by their own yardsticks?

Sort of, in some places. They accomplished a lot of what they wanted to achieve, but in some ways they came up short.

Still, again, I couldn't resist seeing this partial success as strangely appropriate for the project, as a match for the story they were trying to tell. This was a game about a civilization that makes a desperate bid for survival, a Hail Mary trek into the cosmos, responding to a dim signal from deep space prophesied in a book everyone took for fiction. *Of course* it doesn't quite work out. Amazingly, against all odds, the signal turns out to be real, and your civilization manages to detect it. Amazingly, against all odds, you build the ships to get you there. But obviously, when you arrive, things aren't as simple as you'd imagined. The prophecies are incomplete and contradictory. The planet seems unsure whether it wants you there. You begin to question whether your presence there is ethically justifiable – whether you can balance the survival of your civilization against wiping out an entire ecosystem, an entirely different form of intelligence, a whole system of being.

The real action of JETT isn't having your cellphone stolen twice. It's coming to grips with the reality that your civilization's great quest, the one you yourself are helping to lead, is probably going to fail and was probably wrong to begin with. So of course JETT wouldn't just be a slam dunk. Of course it would be a partial success – a triumph in some respects, a failure in others. It was that kind of project because it was *about* that kind of project.

That was something else to hold on to. I picked it up, put it in my other pocket.

I knew what I wanted to say about JETT.

11.

Every fall, I begin my course 'Modern Fiction 1880–1950' with a lecture called 'My Two Theories of Modernism.' The first theory you already know: modernists were the first punks, the first to practise the DIY ethic in the arts, the first to self-consciously capitalize on the power of cheap duplication to write what they wanted, in their own way, at their own length, in their own time, at their own bidding. The second theory has to do with the kinds of art that modernists actually produced – the distinctive works of art that DIY methods enabled them to write, print, and circulate. The second theory is: modernism is dialogism.

The term 'dialogism' comes from Mikhail Bakhtin, the Russian literary theorist. He used it to describe the characteristic multi-voicedness of the novel, as opposed to the single-voiced or 'mono-logic' world of epic poetry. A dialogic novel – Bakhtin was thinking particularly of the novels of Dostoevsky – reflects the real diversity of a democratic public sphere, incorporating all styles and all ideologies, setting them against one another without trying to resolve them into a coherent vision. As Bakhtin wrote in 'Discourse in the Novel,'

> The prose art presumes a deliberate feeling for the historical and social concreteness of living discourse, as well as its relativity, a feeling for its participation in historical becom-ing and in social struggle; it deals with discourse still warm from that struggle and hostility, as yet unresolved and still fraught with hostile intentions and accents.

This kind of wild, untamed, uncooled, unresolved writing flour-ished in the modernist period for several reasons. It was a time of rapid technological change, so that life was changing and becoming unsettled. New transportation and communication technologies were putting individuals as well as entire cultures in touch with one another in unprecedented ways. It was the era of Marx and Nietzsche, Pankhurst and Garvey, Einstein and Freud, so the ideas carried by these new technologies were revolutionary. It was also the era of world war, when contact between cultures was violent and extreme. The multi-voiced, unresolved, untamed dialogic novel reflected the upheavals of modernism. As another important critic of dialogism, Erich Auerbach, wrote in *Mimesis*,

> It is easy to understand that such a technique had to develop gradually and that it did so precisely during the decades of the first World War and after. The widening of man's horizon, and the increase of his experiences, which began in the sixteenth century, continued through the nineteenth at an even faster tempo – with such a tremendous acceleration since the beginning of the twentieth that synthetic and objective attempts at interpretation are produced and demolished every instant.

But the dialogic modernist novel didn't just *reflect* this turmoil, it also made an active intervention in it. There were two possible responses to this turmoil: to engage with it, to ride the wave – or to try to tame it. Modernist art took the former path. Propaganda and authoritarianism, offering simple solutions to complex problems, took the latter. Auerbach writes,

> The temptation to entrust oneself to a sect which solves all problems, whose power of suggestion imposed solidarity, and which ostracized everything that would not fit in and submit – this temptation was so great that, with many people, fascism hardly had to employ force when the time came for it to spread through the countries of old European culture.

Auerbach and Bakhtin both suffered at the hands of authoritarian regimes. Auerbach, a German Jew, was forced into exile during the Second World War, and wrote the above words in Istanbul. Bakhtin formulated dialogism while in Kazakhstan as an internal exile in Stalin's USSR. Both turned to dialogic literature in these circumstances because they believed it made a difference. It did so by training its readers to accept complexity and exist in uncertainty.

The same year that Bakhtin began his major work, 'Discourse in the Novel,' Stalin gave a speech in which he declared that whereas his first Five Year Plan had depended on 'mining engineers, construction engineers, electrical engineers, engineers to build blast furnaces,' the next great step in the development of the Soviet Union would depend on 'engineers who know how to build human souls.' Addressing an audience of novelists, he said, 'Writers, you are the engineers who build human souls!' Modernists saw themselves as the counter-engineers. Authoritarian regimes – and capitalist democracy, too – were developing simple, digestible cultural forms to promote passivity and servitude. Modernists responded with forms that shocked their readers into active, independent reflection and trained them to reject coherence and certainty as ideologically suspect. Dialogic modernist literature, modelling the diversity and disagreement of a healthy body politic, also trained its readers to become comfortable with uncertainty and ambiguity – not to try to resolve all complexity, but to accept it as an essential aspect of living. The reader of a modernist novel complains to its author, 'I don't get it. It's confusing. I'm not sure how I should feel about it. I don't know who to like or which characters are good or evil. I'm not even sure what's happening.' To which the modernist author responds, 'You're welcome.'

Accepting complexity doesn't lead to stasis – to the reader throwing up their hands in despair, giving up – but to a new form of action. Once you've seen that uncertainty is inevitable, the next step is to navigate it. What modernist literature teaches its readers to do, in the words of the philosopher Chantal Mouffe, is to 'decide within an undecidable terrain.' The world is complex and ambiguous; there are no simple answers, no absolutely correct paths. But still, some decisions are better than others, and you need to have the intelligence and the strength and resolve to identify those, commit to them, and carry them through. That is the lesson of modernist fiction – the process that it models.

It is also what JETT models.

That was the first thing I wanted to say about it: that JETT is, in every sense, a modernist game.

The second was that JETT is an allegory.

Allegory in literature feels incredibly old-fashioned. I associate it with centuries-old works like Edmund Spenser's Elizabethan epic *The Faerie Queene*, which I dragged my way through in grad school – a text where Britomart, symbolizing Chastity, jousts with Artegall, symbolizing Justice; where characters restore their spirits in the House of Holiness and the Bower of Bliss; where you encounter a snake puking out a book, and the footnote tells you this represents theological error. In *The Spenser Encyclopedia*, Gordon Teskey defines an allegory as 'a fiction told in such a way as to indicate, by "aptly suggestive resemblance," a clear structure of nonfictional ideas.' In the case of the *The Faerie Queene*, the allegory works on many levels: the adventures of Britomart et al. symbolize virtue at the moral level, the rise of Protestantism on the religious level, the reign of Queen Elizabeth on the political level, and so on. One of the many frustrating things about allegory is that the actual story, the characters you encounter, and the places the action unfolds – all vanish behind these symbolic associations, becoming mere props for the deeper meaning the author has designed them to illustrate. As Teskey puts it, the plot of an allegorical world is presented 'as being secondary to a meaning that the reader must try to recover by engaging in interpretive play.' If you enjoy that kind of thing, great. But most readers today would rather follow a plot that feels realistic and characters who feel human. As such, allegory is generally regarded, as the literary critic Jim Hansen puts it, as the 'clumsiest and most belabored of formal devices.'

Not so in videogames, however. You can still get away with making allegorical games – and these games can in fact become classics, be regarded as pioneering, daring, boundary-crushing masterpieces. One need look no further than the much-discussed *BioShock*, an allegory of Ayn Rand's Objectivist philosophy. Why is this the case – why is allegory still permitted in videogames, when it has been banished as a creative option from the other major arts? Maybe it's because games are still a young form, so that allegory can still feel fresh. Maybe it's because gamers are more comfortable with surfaces that vanish behind their deeper meanings. Every art demands some willing suspension of disbelief, but in videogames – because they are *games* – these demands can be extreme. In *JETT*, as in all narrative games, there are details of the world that you simply can't focus on, or they'll spoil the fun. Isn't it a little too convenient, for instance, that your jett runs on vapour – and that this alien planet just happens to be teeming with the stuff, delivered by plants that grow in shapes that seem specifically designed for your jett to fly through? It's like landing on Mars and finding a bunch of drive-through Esso stations with automatic self-service. It's the same with ion pools, shelters, resin, the laser-shooting spires that surround Tor – you have to accept them for their larger role as mechanics in gameplay, and ignore their plausibility as features of this world, or else you'll drive yourself mad. To enjoy a game, to allow yourself to become immersed in it, you have to learn to see past the literal surface, to accept that meaning is on another level.

Or maybe allegory has remained viable in videogames because, as Gordon Teskey argues, allegory is itself a kind of game. Teskey sees allegory as a form of 'interpretive play' that 'promotes a sustained interaction between reader and text that has many of the features of a game.' As the reader or player of an allegory, your job is to figure out what it means for a snake to be puking out a book, then to string that interpretation together with a thousand others, into some grand theory with moral, historical, and political significance. Interpretation itself becomes a game. Getting it right means recovering the creator's vision, which means you win.

'Resonate' was another favourite term among the JETT team – maybe because they spent their days flying around in little spaceships, scanning the horizon with a tool called a resonator. Luckily for me, it's also the perfect word to describe the reverberations of allegorical symbols at multiple levels of meaning. JETT resonates on at least two.

The literal story that JETT tells – scouts leave their planet to find a new home in Ghoke's dim glow, but in the process of establishing themselves find the planet ambivalent to their presence – offers an allegory, first of all, of environmental destruction. The quick tour we take of their home planet in the Prologue shows us the likely consequences of our own practices of pollution and unchecked resource extraction: if we keep going in the way we are here on earth, our civilization, like theirs, is going to be left with no option but a Hail Mary into the cosmos. As Craig promised it would from the start, the game attempts to 'move the needle' on ecological consciousness – and one of his tools for doing so is allegory.

A second level of allegorical meaning relates to colonialism. JETT's story of apparently enlightened conquest has something to teach us about the legacies of conquest we continue to try to spin as enlightened. Despite the scouts' sense that this distant planet has *invited* them from across the stars, despite their best efforts to be as respectful as possible in exploring this potential new home, they must confront the reality that they are conquerors. 'Time to let slip our masks of innocence,' Mirror Mei says during her vision in the Tor Cleft. 'Time to reckon with who we are. Time to relinquish our hegemonic vision.'

On both these levels, there is something testing and complex about JETT's allegory. Yes, JETT is an allegorical work – but not an old-fashioned one, and not in the usual way.

JETT is a modernist allegory.

Allegory, as it's usually understood, is far from dialogic. In fact, it's about the most monologic setup imaginable: an author constructs a meticulously arranged series of symbolic associations, and your job as a reader is just to figure out what exactly they all mean. The author has all the power: they've scattered the fragments, and you're there to sweep them up and put them back in order. As the critic Bill Brown argues about Dante's *Divine Comedy* – the most famous literary allegory of them all – there is also something authoritarian in the allegorist's urge to trap all the ambivalence of lived experience in a tightly controlled structure. If Dante's project can be seen as 'heroic,' it's in its 'commitment to rendering a totalizing theory concrete, which means enveloping everything in the meaning produced by the perceived world structure.' Brown sees Dante's heroic task as a grand 'act of cognitive mapping,' 'an effort to resolve the ecclesiastical, political, and social disorientations of his world.' Where modernism teaches its readers to exist in uncertainty, to accept complexity as an ineradicable and inescapable condition, allegory pushes in the other direction, selling a myth of perfect correspondences by which chaos can be resolved and everything put in its right place. Rather than making you grapple with the fact that reality is hopelessly complex, allegory gives you a coherent toy to play with – it distracts you from the unfathomable with perfect design.

For Gordon Teskey, though, that's not how the game of allegory actually works in practice. Yes, the author might have some grand multi-levelled structure of allegory in mind – some perfectly neat architecture in which to resolve all the turmoil of existence. But real-life readers can never quite keep up. Just when they've got a handle on the book-vomiting serpent, there's a milk-white mare coming over the horizon, or a pig walking on its hind legs.

Teskey says that readers are pushed along in an allegory by the promise that eventually all these mysterious signs will be sorted out – that all the confusion will dissolve into a beatific vision. But the moment never comes, not even in Dante. At the end of the *Divine Comedy*, Teskey says, 'instead of being offered a disclosure of what all the previous signs mean, we are confronted with a new collocation of symbols indicating that the truth to which they point is too sublime ever to be comprehended.' This is not a quirk of Dante's style, he says, but the 'distinctive effect' of every allegory, which is 'to regulate the scope of interpretation without coming to a definitive end.' For Teskey, allegory is a bizarre game where the winning condition – understanding – can never be fulfilled. And that's the point, he says: like the dialogic modernist novel, the *purpose* of the game is training its players how to live in the world, where survival and sanity depend on trying as hard as you possibly can to understand what's around you while also coming to grips with the fact that full comprehension is an unreachable end.

It's a brilliant conception, but not entirely original. In seeing allegory as fundamentally broken – as fundamentally *about* brokenness – Teskey is following Walter Benjamin.

Clearly, I have a thing for German philosophers who torpedo their academic careers by refusing to put footnotes in their first books. Nietzsche's *Birth of Tragedy* – published in 1872 with nary a note – had allowed me to unlock *Sworcery*. Now Walter Benjamin's *Origin of the German Tragic Drama* – submitted citation-free, and rejected by his dissertation committee, in 1925 – held the keys to JETT.

Benjamin's book is a dense and mysterious study of an extraordinarily obscure literary form: the German 'mourning play' of the baroque period. Benjamin focuses on the minor works of forgotten playwrights: complex allegorical plays obsessed with aristocratic intrigues that the world has long since forgotten. The allegories that these plays present are *broken*: the symbols don't make sense unless you know all the players and all the controversies in, say, the Silesian court of 1662 – which is to say, to a contemporary reader, they don't make any sense at all, and they never will. But as with Teskey, this brokenness strikes Benjamin as essential, both to the baroque allegories in particular and to allegories in general. Eventually, Benjamin says, *every* allegory will end up like the ones in these obscure plays: all the intrigues in all the courts in all the world ever, which all seem so absolutely crucial at the time – all these will be forgotten. Every allegorical system will eventually collapse, will become like a dead language, a set of signifiers pointing to signifieds that have vanished – a bunch of broken links. As Benjamin says, 'Allegories are, in the realm of thoughts, what ruins are in the realm of things.' The collapsed structure of a dead allegory, like the ruin of a temple, reminds us of the ravages of time, the inevitability of decline, the fact that all things must pass. (The place you live, the seat you're sitting in as you read this book, this book, this game – all ruins in time.) To encounter a broken allegory is to experience the contrast in P. B. Shelley's poem 'Ozymandias': a sculpture of a king with a proud inscription, 'Look on my Works, ye Mighty, and despair!' – abandoned, ruined, set in nothingness: 'Round the decay / Of that colossal Wreck, boundless and bare / The lone and level sands stretch far away.' As Jim Hansen says, 'Allegory becomes the formal feature par excellence of the transient and the irretrievable. It points not to redemption, but only to the Fall itself, only to the dated and the worldly.'

Benjamin's interpretation of allegory couldn't be further from that of Bill Brown. For Brown, allegory is a desperate attempt to redeem the fallen world by organizing it into a meticulous, indomitable structure. For Benjamin, the lesson of allegory is inevitable decay. It exposes the futility of grand narratives of progress, conquest, and divine right – all, like Ozymandias, bound to end in ruin, as ruins. As Hansen puts it, for Benjamin 'history resembles something like a series of ruins, rather than a progressive *Geist* or consciousness, and is much more accurately mourned as a collection of lost and defeated cultures than celebrated as a triumphal procession from the past into the future.'

Running my Benjaminian theory by the various members of the JETT Squad, I was happy to find that it resonated with them, though in different ways.

For Patrick, the idea of ruins evoked all the abandoned ideas that still lurked in forgotten corners of the game. 'There is a lot of vestigial stuff' in JETT, he said, 'little remnants of things.' For instance, at one time they put a lot of effort into a creature called a 'rock hopper' who unburrows himself and tries to steal repair gems – 'and if you try to repair, he spits at you.' All the rock hoppers had been removed from the game years before – but in August of 2021, as they were getting ready to ship, Zack Wheeler, JETT's QA lead, found one floating in the air. Patrick liked the way that these vestiges of forgotten ideas, though unintentional, gave the world a sense of depth – made it seem less like a deliberately created thing, more like an accidental product of history. 'That aspect is cool and fun,' Patrick said, 'to have a creature that *may or may not exist!*'

To other members of the team, my ideas about allegory led to reflections about the way that art sometimes works best when it is suggestive without insisting on specific meanings. Benjamin's ruins reminded art director Sam Bradley of David Lynch, whose work presents 'a sensory experience meant to *evoke something*' but doesn't insist on 'a literal narrative.' He reflected that he and Craig had taken a Lynchian approach to the announce trailer, which was meant to inspire 'pleasant confusion,' a feeling of 'I don't know what this game is, but I want to play it.'

For Andy – a devoted sci-fi fan who often found himself frustrated with the genre's too-obvious allegories – the key Benjaminian sequence in JETT was Mei's encounter in the Tor Cleft. It evoked scenes in classic sci-fi where an alien intelligence communicates with humans through familiar objects, the most on-the-nose example being the beach scene in *Contact* in which aliens present themselves to Jodie Foster's character in the form of her dead father. Something similar is happening in the Cleft, Andy thinks: when the 'Steppe Chorus' song plays here, repeated from the start of the game, it's as if 'Tor has dug through the explorers' brains and found this and so it's singing this back, like "This is a thing that's important to you and you'd like."' But the allegory is far less straightforward, much less resolvable, in JETT than in *Contact*. Andy summarized his reaction to Mei's vision: 'What the heck's going on here? Is she dreaming? Sort of? I guess? But this thing's influencing her dreams? Where are we?' The answers to these questions 'just aren't relevant, in deference to the experience of it.' He added, 'I'm fine with allegory in movies and books. But a lot of that is just like, "This looks cool as shit!" Like [Jodorowsky's] *Holy Mountain* is one of my favourite movies. I don't know *anything* about the meaning of all that. You know that every single thing is some symbolic thing. I'm just like, "It just *looks* cool."'

That's how allegory works in JETT: as a cool, beautiful, irresolvable ruin. The art is evocative and avoids pinning down absolute meanings. The world is rich and dense in a way that embraces and incorporates some of the randomness and mystery of the natural world.

And also, in the simplest, most literal way, we encounter JETT's world as a series of ruins.

Emerging from the yurt at the start of the game, we do not, and cannot, understand the symbols that surround us: the trigons, the stag's heads, the winged sculptures, the hot-air balloons, the kolos gates, the giant statues of upturned hands. What is a mystic? What is an anchorite? What do the obscure symbols and diagrams that we encounter in the pages of Tsosi's tsagas actually mean? They all clearly mean something, but their meanings are as obscure to us as the allegories in a baroque mourning play. Meaning is elsewhere; meaning is on another level. They're all dead links.

We don't know what they mean – and we will never figure them out, because this civilization has destroyed itself. By the time the scouts reach the far shore, the home they leave in the Prologue is literally a ruin, existing only as broken symbols in their memories and 'remnant dreams.'

The lesson of allegory in JETT is exactly as Benjamin perceived: that history is not a triumphal march toward some glorious destination, but a collection of lost and defeated cultures.

Well, maybe 'lesson' is too strong a word – because what can you really *do* with an insight like that? For me, modernism isn't just about *telling* the reader that the world is uncertain; it is also about providing them with strategies for *living* in this uncertain world. It doesn't just present elegant proof that the terrain of existence is undecidable – it also shows you that, however difficult, navigating this impossible terrain is also necessary. To use Rancière's terminology, it also drafts maps.

When I discussed my ideas about *Sworcery* with Craig back in 2013, I'd mentioned Ian Bogost's theory of 'procedural rhetoric' – the idea that the power of games is their ability to convince through *action*; that rather than showing or telling you something, they make you actually *do* it. Gordon Teskey makes a similar point about the game of allegory. Teskey quotes Spenser's claim that *The Faerie Queene* would 'fashion' its reader in 'virtuous and gentle discipline.' 'The reader is to be morally changed not just by seeing examples of admirable conduct,' Teskey says, 'but by becoming engaged, through the play of interpretation, in the theory of virtue.'

What change could the player of JETT expect to undergo, working through its uncertain, broken Benjaminian allegory? I think the best single word might be another of Craig's favourites, 'groundedness': a modest, steady, decidedly fallen, historical way of thinking and acting, suited to a decidedly fallen world at a particular moment in history – ours, now.

When he was preparing the final script for JETT, Craig had three main reference points. Writing out every line of dialogue, he would ask himself whether it was more Tolstoy, more *Moby Dick*, or more *The Right Stuff*.

But when I played through to the end of JETT, I was reminded of something else entirely: Book XII of Milton's *Paradise Lost*.

Milton's epic poem, first published in 1667, comes from the same historical period as Benjamin's beloved mourning plays, but it has survived much better. In part that's because it's not an obscure allegory: it retells the story of the fall of Adam and Eve and their expulsion from the Garden of Eden – the very subject of Craig's earliest videogame sketches and magazine illustrations. *Paradise Lost* has also survived because its ideas about time and history are so strikingly modern, and so perfectly anticipate those of Benjamin.

Book XII is the last in the poem. Adam and Eve are about to be expelled from the Garden. The fallen world, earthly history, the world as we know it, is about to begin. Adam is upset at the situation he finds himself in, worried about the future that awaits him. The Archangel Michael doesn't make things any better by giving Adam a full summary of that future, in all its gory detail: a start-to-finish accounting of what Adam's progeny (i.e., humanity) will get up to from the time of the expulsion to the Second Coming. (As a divine being, Michael can see into the fullness of time; Adam, as a mere human, cannot.) The story Michael tells is depressing: war, tyranny, betrayal, injustice. Every now and then, Adam sees some bright thread in the narrative and tries to pull on it. He's still stuck in what Benjamin would call a Messianic mindset: he's still looking for a divine order in everything, he hasn't internalized the randomness and ruin of time, he keeps expecting a climax, a moment when God will reveal His purpose and Adam will be able to say, 'Okay, so *that's* what all this suffering is for! It all works out in the end!' In other words, he's looking for that moment of revelation that Gordon Teskey says allegory is always promising the reader, but which never arrives. Adam thus gets very excited when Michael describes Jesus. 'Needs must the Serpent now his capital bruise / Expect with mortal pain,' says Adam, imagining history ending with Marvel-movie clarity, his personal enemy vanquished in a gnarly tussle. But Michael tells him to stop dreaming of boss battles that solve everything. 'Dream not of their fight, / As of a duel,' Michael says to Adam. Jesus's victory over Satan is painful and incomplete. After he suffers and dies, for the sins of all your descendants, history carries right on in all its randomness and cruelty, right into the dreadful present. (And well beyond Milton's time – here we are today.)

Eventually, Adam gets it: there will be no happy ending. Hope for the future, fine – but be sure to curb your enthusiasm, and place the target of your hope well beyond the horizon of your own life. Adam finally understands the situation: things are grim for Eve and him, they're going to be grim for his children, and their children's children, for eons and eons. There might eventually be a Second Coming, but that's the furthest horizon of all. Adam takes from Michael's story what Benjamin takes from the brokenness of allegory: that history isn't going to be a steady triumphal march, more like a series of catastrophes. But, crucially, this isn't an endpoint for Adam. It's an existential truth – but still, you have to keep going. How do you respond to the collapse of a perfect world? What attitude do you bring with you into a fallen one? As Adam puts it,

> with good
> Still overcoming evil, and by small
> Accomplishing great things, by things deemed weak
> Subverting worldly strong, and worldly wise
> By simply meek: that suffering for truth's sake
> Is fortitude to highest victory.

In other words, you ground yourself: narrow your vision, focus on what you control, do your best, prepare yourself for hard times and don't naïvely expect them to suddenly pass. When Michael hears Adam's words, he tells him he's got it. 'This having learnt, thou hast attained the sum / Of wisdom.' Adam goes off and finds Eve, who's been sleeping. He tells her about the story and the lesson, and off they head, weary but resolute, into the world. 'Some natural tears they dropped, but wiped them soon'; 'They hand in hand with wand'ring steps and slow, / Through Eden took their solitary way.'

So ends *Paradise Lost*. And so, it seemed to me, ends JETT.

I always thought I would be there at JETT's key moments – announce, maybe at GDC; launch, maybe at some huge party in Montreal – getting to speak to the crew at each milestone, collecting their impressions, sharing my thoughts. And I always hoped I'd be able to visit Craig again in the woods of Quebec, once I'd figured out my grand theory of JETT. I pictured following his footsteps up The Summit, delivering it to the back of his red Gore-Tex jacket, worrying that it was all completely in my head, that it was all totally off base, but having no sightline to his reaction, no feedback system to measure the absurdity of my take. If I'd been able to go, I would have said all the stuff in this chapter: Mikhail Bakhtin, Chantal Mouffe, Walter Benjamin, Adam and Eve; existing in uncertainty, deciding within an undecidable terrain, ruins, accomplishing the great through the small, groundedness.

What with the pandemic, and overwhelm, and Craig having nineteen jobs to do, none of that ever happened. But I did get a chance to run some of these ideas by Craig in what had become, by then, our usual way – on Skype (or rather, since nobody used that once-ubiquitous application anymore, on Zoom). I hadn't worked them all out by the time we talked, but I gave him a rough draft. I was relieved to see that what I said resonated.

It resonated at the high level, with fundamental ambitions of the project. From the outset, Craig said, the game was going to be 'about the future, and thinking about the future, and struggling with the complexity of that, and not necessarily resolving anything.' The story of JETT, he said, 'would just be a record of that honest struggle with those themes.'

It also resonated deeper down, on both the allegorical levels of ecology and empire.

Milton's take on Adam and Eve, his insistence on the necessity of taking concrete but modest action in the here and now, got Craig thinking about a fundamental difference between himself and many of his favourite sci-fi authors.

Some people might play JETT and think it was advocating an escape from Planet Earth – that given the bleak prognosis for life here at home, it was arguing that settling elsewhere was the way forward. 'I actually do not view things from that perspective at all,' he said. 'I'm occasionally gripped with the urge to decry that perspective, especially to your Elon Musks or your Jeff Bezoses. It's like, "Hey, shut the fuck up, it's not helpful!": any of that thinking, to me, is aggravatingly naïve.' It wasn't just the Musks and Bezoses: it was also Carl Sagan, and other thinkers he respected.

> There's this kind of humility of, 'Oh, we're just one little planet, we're a pale blue dot at the corner of an inconsequential galaxy.' And I understand this kind of reverent feeling we have for the cosmos, and the smallness that we feel as this pale blue dot. And I think that as a counterbalance to what came before, where the whole universe revolved around the earth, that it's an important exercise, an important correction. But there's got to be a middle space that acknowledges that this planet, for all we know now and all we'll ever know, is the most remarkable thing, until further notice.

Although Craig acknowledged that JETT told the tale of such a moon shot, it was not one that he endorsed. 'No,' he said,

> I believe that our species is not ever going to progress beyond Earth, because, why would we? It's foolish. Where are we going to go? To Mars? That place is not a habitable

planet. It's a place to die. Every other place is a place to die. Are you now going to cross the depths of space and find another place to die? None of this stuff is even interesting to consider, I feel.

'There's this humility,' he said, 'and this naïveté that allows people to look beyond our planet and dream, and I feel like that's just extraordinarily unhelpful when what's needed is for us to look in the mirror and see who we are as a species and see what we're doing around us.' It was Milton's point, or one of them. Adam is hopelessly naïve for thinking that the trouble he finds himself in will be miraculously solved by a moon shot or a *deus ex machina*. What you need to do is grapple with the harm you've done, then take modest and responsible action in the here and now. As Mirror Mei puts it, 'Time to reckon with who we are.'

Craig's thoughts on imperialism were in a similar vein. At the start of the project – at the same time he was digging into classic science fiction – he was also traversing 'the history of discovery and the New World.' There were, he saw, two ways of approaching these narratives. On the one hand, 'You can focus on the veneer of, "Wow! It's interesting to cross a large expanse and to see different permutations of life,"' and there was a 'specific awakening' that might come from these kinds of encounters. But at the same time, he said, you can't let this obscure the fact that 'you are riding on top of this machine that is going to destroy what it finds and use it up for the purpose of sustaining a comfortable life':

> For *Star Trek*, you can try to keep focus on this kind of scientific awakening aspect. But even if you try to do that, it's still riding the same dynamics. It's still imperial, it's still what it is. So with this story, we weren't going to pin the problems that are just built into the human experience onto a villain or a plot. None of the characters end up being a villain. All of the characters are doing their best. That's not the issue. They are attempting to make the right

decisions case by case. But it's not enough, because there are some fundamentals to settling on a planet, and there are consequences, and you can only fool yourself so far. And the scouts themselves struggle with that. Like Isao.

Craig and Randy were aligned on a crucial point about JETT: that its most important moment comes after the scouts have finally synchronized the datacore, when Isao takes Mei aside for a chat.

Although the scouts have just accomplished their mission, Isao's mood is far from triumphant. Instead, he's deeply ambivalent. He's been that way throughout the game – warning you to tread lightly, scolding you when you pop too close to a hoppa, blaming himself for provoking the planet by planting a spike. After the battle with the ocean kolos, Isao had told Mei, 'This isn't who I thought we'd be.' Now he asks her a question. 'Looking ahead to our future,' he says, 'I wonder. What should our people do?' It's one of very few choice nodes that the player is given in JETT, and there are three options: 'strive to flourish, whatever the consequences,' 'abdicate – allow oblivion to outpace us, and thus limit our harm,' or 'stumble haphazardly forward, with reverent spirit.' You only get one chance to answer; there is no going back.

Randy described this to me as one of the few times that a videogame – even a critically vaunted one – had ever asked him a serious moral question:

> Normally in a videogame like *BioShock* or whatever, when the game is like, 'Well, do you want to kill this little girl or not?' I'm like, 'Are you seriously posing this as a fucking moral choice? Just because I'm like Edward Pistolhands and the only verb I have to interact with the world is killing things?' Is it good or bad to kill a little girl?? Like, this is not a moral decision!

Isao's question prompted one of the few instances Randy could recall in which he needed to hit pause and really think about his response.

> It's not because *I* did something wrong that I wound up in this terrible situation. It just *is* an impossible situation. So I like the question from Isao for that reason. That it's sort of like, there is no good answer – but that is what's being asked by this work.

Randy's right: there really is no good answer. Whatever option you choose – and I know, because I played my way back to this scene until I'd explored them all – Isao is left unsatisfied. Strive to flourish? 'If we survive, and if we then thrive … what then?' Abdicate? 'To come all this way, only to give up. It seems absurd. Still – if we were to suddenly relent, if our people were to perish … this pristine planet would remain as it is now.' Stumble forward? 'It does not inspire. A path heavy with regret. Also the path most travelled.' As Craig sees it, the choice isn't really yours, or Mei's, anyway. The way Craig reads Isao,

> He's just a sort of helpful friend, and he kind of grows on you as things go on. And then as things twist and turn toward the end, he feels it. And then there's that sort of coda moment, where he engages you in conversation. But it's not as if what he says is a twist or a curve ball or a revelation. It's just a little window into how he's struggling, and the various forms of unsatisfactory compromise that he's trying to comfort himself with.

The struggle is his – and the forms of compromise, however unsatisfactory, are in the end just idle speculations. Even if you sympathize with him, in your heart you know – and he knows – that there isn't really much choice, that you won't actually abdicate, and you probably won't flourish. You'll probably just stumble forward – which is probably why that choice seems to irritate him so much. 'Even if you put yourself in his shoes,' Craig said,

> you're struggling with this, but you do need to put one foot in front of the other. You've got that operating system around you. Are you going to choose to break with it? Or are you going to choose to put one foot in front of the other for the good of your friends? Who you love? Even while you can see this coming and you know what's up?

It was Adam and Eve leaving the garden. It was deciding within an undecidable terrain.

As Craig spoke these words, working through his empathy for this character he had created, I wondered who the 'you' was.

The last question I asked Craig was whether JETT had a third level of allegory. Maybe he and the JETT Squad were the scouts. Having now completed their mission – rescued their cellphones from that pesky kolos, twice – and endured all kinds of existential crises along the way, they were headed back to Ground Control, ambivalent and with heavy hearts, getting ready for another thousand-year sleep. Was JETT's story also the story of its creation?

He let out an exhausted chuckle, like he hadn't really thought of it before.

> Those scouts, they did their best. They had good hearts, good spirits, they were skilful. But, it was a tough predicament and there was no way to earn a *clear* victory. But they survived, they did what needed to be done in the short term, and so, with a relatively clear conscience and a fair bit of exhaustion, they are putting themselves into torpor with an uncertain future but some faith … yeah, a hopefulness that there's something on the other side of torpor. And yeah, that's where we're all at: Patrick and I and everybody.

EPILOGUE

Somewhere in *The Sublime Object of Ideology* – a book I became totally obsessed with in my early twenties – the Slovenian philosopher Slavoj Žižek talks about the curious way that meaning 'comes from the future.' He makes the point in the course of a fairly technical discussion of Lacanian psychoanalysis and Walter Benjamin's 'Theses on the Philosophy of History,' but the idea is transportable to other contexts. It goes something like this: any given point in time, as you're experiencing it, doesn't mean anything yet – it's just raw material, yet to be wrapped up into the stories that will give it significance. You meet a stranger, you fall flat on your face, you see a rainbow on the horizon: as they're happening, they're just moments, fleeting and transitory. They will only become *events* later, based on what comes next, based on the needs and desires of some future self who looks back on them, interpreting them retroactively. The present is empty. Meaning returns from the future.

It's one of my favourite things to think about, and it's the basis of my favourite passage of literary criticism – the following one from Erich Auerbach's *Mimesis*:

> There is always going on within us a process of formulation and interpretation whose subject matter is our own self. We are constantly endeavoring to give meaning and order to our lives in the past, the present, and the future, to our surroundings, the world in which we live; with the result that our lives appear in our own conception as total entities – which to be sure are always changing, more or less radically, more or less rapidly, depending on the extent to

which we are obliged, inclined, and able to assimilate the onrush of new experience.

Not only does meaning return from the future, it arrives from *every* future. The process is permanent and ongoing. You notice it most when you arrive at some new milestones in your life or experience some trauma. But it's *always* happening – we're *constantly* rearranging our past moments into a narrative that explains and justifies where we are now and where we think we're going next.

After spending many decades trying to figure out why literature means so much to me, this is the best explanation I've come across. It's because we're narrative-building machines, because our happiness and our health depend so much on our ability to build good stories, because we're always looking for new examples, new strategies for reaching back into our pasts and lining things up so as to propel us into the future.

As I write these words, it is 7:03 on the morning of Monday, October 4th, 2021. In a little under two hours, the embargo on reviews of JETT will be lifted, and we'll finally see what the critics think of it. This evening, I'll join the JETT Squad's pre-launch celebration on Zoom – if Craig remembers to send me the link, that is. Then, as the clock strikes midnight, as the needle pushes over into a new day, JETT will launch for PlayStation, and then nine hours later in the Epic Game Store.

For the first time on this project, Craig and I are relatively aligned. We've both finished our work, and are just waiting for it to come out. Over the past few months, I've recreated in miniature the hectic experience of JETT's final years. After a relaxed but meandering initial phase – long and sometimes aimless – things have gotten intense as I've shifted into pragmatic production. We've even ramped up, in our own small way. For years it was just me, but now there's a team editing, designing, laying-out, fact-checking, and supervising. I'm tired: I've been getting up early to do my writing before heading off to teach each day, then staying up late editing, reading, organizing, thinking, worrying. I haven't been in hell: I've loved the focus that comes with pressure, enjoyed the effort, and loved the comradeship of working with a team, something I don't often get to experience. It's only been intense for a couple of months, and the finish line has always been in sight. It's been enough for me to understand some of what Craig went through. But still, it isn't the same. Eight years of this? I don't know how he did it. We are aligned only to a point.

And in a few hours, we'll shift back out of phase completely. The next couple of days won't determine what JETT is forever and all time. Initial reactions are often wildly off-base, as Woolf wrote, and as she knew. She wasn't taken very seriously in her own time, and after her death she was known as an eccentric female chronicler of London high society. It wasn't until critics like Erich Auerbach came around that the tide was turned, that she was recognized and established as a classic. As Bourdieu put it, 'The production of discourse about a work of art is part of the production of a work of art.' That process is just as fraught as the one by which art itself is created.

If JETT is destined to be a classic, the definitive indie game of 2021, the game of the century, the magnum opus of our civilization – or just a game some people liked, others didn't care for, most didn't notice – whatever the case, it won't be decided right away.

Still, today marks the start of the process. Once it's out, it begins its shift from moment to event, from raw material to something with a meaning. The future is coming for *The Future*.

At 8:59, I send Craig a text message – 'Big moment,' and the crossed fingers emoji. Then at 9:00 I start checking the big sites for reviews (IGN, *Polygon*, *Gamespot*). Nothing yet.

When I try Metacritic, JETT is on their front page. I click, and it already has a metascore! Seventy-five: right on the threshold for 'generally favourable reviews.' I follow the links to all the ones written in English – many are from Europe, due to time zones –

and devour them. They are all in publications I haven't heard of, many of which I wouldn't know how to pronounce. *Wccftech* declares JETT 'a genuine work of art,' correctly notes that it 'walks a delicate line between optimism and hopelessness,' but complains that although they 'get that non-violence is an important theme of this game,' sometimes they wished they 'could just blast some shit.' Balancing similar extremes, *Hey Poor Player* says JETT 'provides a truly otherworldly experience,' is 'unlike anything I've played,' but also repeatedly 'made me want to throw my controller.' *Inverse* gives JETT a 90 percent and has the best title: '2021's Dreamiest Existential Crisis.'

But, curiously, the reviews that give JETT high scores often don't seem to really get it, and vice versa. *Screen Rant* praises JETT for capturing 'the epic grandeur of exploring space' with 'a fun and complex flight model' – both assessments are about half-right, missing the angst of exploration and the frustration and vulnerability of slow-speed flight. The smartest review is the one that gives JETT the lowest score, a sixty-seven; it's from *Player 2* in Australia. The review has a leitmotif: every paragraph ends with some variation on the theme 'Presumably. Perhaps. Maybe? Maybe not?' They find JETT's world 'completely alien yet fully self-assured; a place that feels just as much unearthed as it does created.' It plays at times like 'an early generational classic.' The only problem is that it ends too soon: 'just as all of the pieces seem poised to truly deliver, it's all over.' They love it so much that 'it almost hurts that there is no "Part One" in the title.' And this is the *worst* review!

Now it's 10 a.m., and I reload the Metacritic page. Bad news: the metascore has tumbled to sixty-five, 'mixed or average reviews.' This time I know the names of the publications. They don't like JETT.

Gamespot, the first of the big sites to weigh in, has given it a fifty. The puzzles are boring and the game never gives you a chance to sort them out for yourself. The so-called 'read/fly problem' – an issue Craig, Patrick, and Randy had been trying to solve for years – is rearing its ugly head: because the game is in an incomprehensible language requiring subtitles, it often delivers written instructions during moments of high tension. And, *Gamespot* notes, 'there's a very clear reason folks in the real world aren't allowed to read text messages while driving.' Even worse is the emptiness and passivity of Mei's character. Although people are constantly talking at her, she 'doesn't get a chance to express how she feels.' Even at the end of the game, the *Gamespot* reviewer still isn't 'sure what her motivations were for joining the mission and why she chose to fight so hard to ensure it would succeed.'

For some reason this has never occurred to me, this voicelessness of Mei. But it's at the heart of another negative review. This one's in the NME – the essential British magazine of the post-punk eighties, which I see is now reviewing games. Mei, the NME complains, 'is a silent protagonist': the reviewer, thinking aloud from Mei's perspective, says 'I did a lot of good work for the team, but was I ever really one of them?'

Now it is 10:25, and I need to head to campus to teach my 11 a.m. class. But I'm feeling personally wounded by these reviews, as if the game were mine. I expected mixed reviews, but these feel unfair and harsh.

I ask myself: What if the game really *is* this bad? What if I've spent eight years, and pretty much every waking second of the past two months, writing a book about a total flop? I start imagining the reviews for this book. 'No amount of Walter Benjamin will save this terrible game – turn its bad design into deep meaning, its boring plot into some kind of brilliant discourse on boredom.'

I'm reloading Metacritic, hoping the score will jump, turn up some rave in a major publication that will banish my gloom and justify all my effort. There's nothing new – just the same reviews, the same sixty-four. But on a whim I go to polygon.com, to see if they've posted something that Metacritic hasn't uploaded … And they have! Title: 'JETT: *The Far Shore* puts the majesty back in space travel.' Subtitle: 'An awe-inspiring odyssey.' Long exhale. But now I'll really be late for class; I have to go.

It's 12:15, and I'm walking back home from campus. I have just given a one-hour lecture on *Dr. Jekyll and Mr. Hyde*. Naturally, I have argued that Robert Louis Stevenson – from a long line of Scottish lighthouse engineers – is *a lighthouse engineer of human souls*, training his readers to inhabit the uncertain spaces between absolute binaries of good and evil.

Just before I get home, Craig texts with the Zoom link to the launch party. I reply, telling him I'm about to dig into the *Polygon* review. I can't resist adding, 'I keep reading the other reviews and thinking arrrrrgh, just read the last chapter of my book!! Some projects are genuinely, actually ABOUT ambivalence!!' It is Robert Louis Stevenson's point: seriously, it's possible to feel two things at the same time.

I read the *Polygon* review, and it is both very positive and deeply smart. 'While other games focus on the danger or the adventure of interstellar travel, JETT places all of its emphasis on the unsettling, awe-inspiring, and utterly alien beauty of it all.' Precisely! JETT 'isn't comforting; at times, it's sad and even bleak.' Yes! And these are reasons to *like* the game, to give it a *high* score!

Two more reviews have come in while I've been out. *WellPlayed* says JETT has 'all the right ingredients for a cult indie success' but says its 'egregious wordiness' (hypocrite!), 'need to have the intellectual high ground,' and 'clumsy controls' in fact make it 'one of the most disappointing … indie games of the year.'

PC *Gamer* weighs in with more complaints about those clumsy controls: 'Thank Christ my co-pilot … is a chill dude because I'm crashing into cliffs, getting snagged on rocks, and caught in various vegetation.' I realize that my lack of gaming expertise has been a real advantage in navigating JETT: seeing myself as an alien presence in the world of glossy flying games, I was able to take the game for what it is, not to expect it to behave like all my other favourites.

PC *Gamer*'s verdict is that JETT 'has some epic highs but fiddly ship controls and unanswered questions weigh this space adventure down.' But unanswered questions are what this game is all about! Haven't you read Stevenson? Haven't you read my book??

On that note, Craig finally responds to my earlier text, the one where I explained that his game is *about* ambivalence. 'Haha,' he writes, 'it is what it is. Could be some other shoe still to drop, but as of now it feels like this is as good a rollout as JETT could have had.'

'We seem to be on a good path towards a cult classic,' he adds, 'unusual and fascinating.' I say that's fine with me, that my book certainly makes more sense as one about a cult classic rather than a blockbuster. 'Sure am glad we avoided the blockbuster trap,' Craig replies, 'wouldn't want to go mainstream, haha.'

It is now 7 p.m, T-minus one hour to the JETT Squad's Eve of Launch Hangout. Fifty-two reviews have been recorded in the spreadsheet that Popagenda, JETT's marketing firm, has helpfully shared with me. I have read them all – printed them all out, in fact, and highlighted all the important bits.

But the headlines are sufficient to tell the tale. Some reviews are very good: 'It's too soon to call it but JETT: *The Far Shore* could be another all timer from Superbrothers' (*Glasshouse.games*). Some are very bad: 'To Boldly Go Nowhere' (*Game Informer*). Most are pointedly ambivalent: 'A Flawed Masterpiece' (*GameCrater*); 'Stark, Beautiful, and Frustrating' (*Uppercut Critic*); 'A profound but extremely irritating space odyssey' (*Eurogamer* UK). If there is anything like a critical consensus about JETT on its first day, it runs as follows: that it is brilliant but awful, amazing but shit. (Woolf was not wrong about the way that new works of art are received by their contemporaries.)

The most piercing review of this latest batch sees JETT's ambivalence not as a feature, as my own analysis did, but as a genuine bug. *Rock Paper Shotgun* says the game is 'at war with itself,' trying to present both 'a tightly controlled, linear gallery of gorgeous vignettes' and 'an experimental pool for playing with an alien ecosystem.' It's not only the far shore that is 'at odds with itself,' as Jones says in the game; it's also *The Far Shore*, tying itself in knots to be two mutually exclusive things at the same time. It's not ambivalent, RPS says, it's incoherent.

As I am writing this up before the launch party, I get another text from Craig. It's a screenshot of the metascore for JETT – sixty-five – followed by a grimacing face, the 'eek' emoji. I note that *Polygon*'s rave has not yet been included. 'It's like watching election results,' he says. 'Just gotta wait for dust to settle, I guess.'

After struggling to get the Zoom link to copy from my phone to my desktop, I join the party slightly late, at 8:05 p.m. Mack is the host and his screen is shared: Sam Bradley's painting of Mei in her space suit, which, we are told, will also be the cover of Andy's soundtrack.

A conversation is underway. It's a good time for indie games, a Squad member says – all the triple-As are dropping the ball. It's our turn. Someone takes the bait: you'd think with all that money, they'd sometimes take just a *bit* of a risk. Videogames are about *experiences*, the first voice replies – so there should be *new* experiences! The 'era of people stroking their beards and talking about stuff' persists.

We all wait for the stragglers, among them Craig. We all find the Zoom setting that allows us to see everyone – there are thirty-two of us – on one screen. Then Craig joins, and there are speeches. Patrick goes first, says this feels great, that it's nice to see so many people, including many he has never met before, thanks everyone. It is a very sincere speech that lasts about one minute. Craig goes next, shifting in his chair and looking uncertain. He notes that Randy can't join because he's in Europe on his honeymoon, then gives a brief history of the game, says he's glad it's resonating with *some* reviewers, and thanks everyone for their efforts. 'And after this, we sort of scatter to the winds,' says Craig.

There are more speeches. Andy says, 'I knew we'd get somewhere great, and I really feel we have.' Other people have their say. Everyone seems a little defensive, a little on edge. They've read the reviews.

But the mood shifts when Gordon McGladdery, studio director of the audio vendor A Shell in the Pit, takes the microphone. He recalls the impact that *Sworcery* had on him when it first came out, how it started him on his path. He doesn't consider himself a gamer: it was the indie-games scene specifically that drew him in. So it was a real honour to be asked to work with a developer who helped solidify his vision of what indie games are and could be. He thanks Craig and Patrick for giving him a big creative leash, to make a game sound exactly the way he wanted it to.

The good vibes continue when Priscilla Snow gives a little toast in Volega, the language they created for the game. Then it's Mack's turn. He's wearing a suit and tie. 'Hi, I'm Mack, I cosplay as the CEO of a videogame company.' He says he's happy this day has arrived, that he wasn't always sure it would. Sarah doesn't give a speech, but she shows us her shoes, pink Chuck Taylors, a reference to something in the game.

After the speeches, Mack shows the launch trailer. Then it's time to wrap things up.

'Who knows where it goes from here?' Craig says.

The call ends. One hundred minutes later, JETT launches.

In the spring of 2013, Patrick McAllister, a.k.a Pine Scented, quit his job as a programmer at the Tokyo-based videogame company Koei. This meant that he and his friend Craig D. Adams, a.k.a. Superbrothers – an artist and game designer who had shipped the hit indie game *Sword & Sworcery* two years before – could now begin full-time work on the joint venture they had long been planning, an ambitious videogame project they called *The Future*. Decision made, job quit, full-time work begun, that's what the project then became: their future.

Their work methods allow us to make a fairly precise estimate of the amount of time each then spent on the project. Because Patrick was in Japan and Craig in the woods of rural Quebec – because they found themselves almost exactly on opposite sides of the planet – they divided the day between them. When the sun was shining in Tokyo, Patrick was working; when there was daylight in the Eastern Townships, it was Craig's turn. Over three thousand days passed between the start of full-time work and the game's launch. That puts the total work hours on the project at around 72,000, about 36,000 each.

As the clock struck midnight on October 5th, 2021, the game was released. With that, the future that began in the spring of 2013 was over. *The Future* was done, it was out in the world. Its meaning was out of their hands; it would return from the future.

WORKS CITED

Anthropy, Anna. *Rise of the Videogame Zinesters*. New York: Seven Stories Press, 2012.

Auerbach, Erich. *Mimesis*. Trans. Willard R. Trask. Princeton, NJ: Princeton University Press, 1953.

Bakhtin, Mikhail Mikhailovich. 'Art and Answerability.' *Art and Answerability*. Ed. Michael Holquist and Vadim Liapunov. Austin: University of Texas Press, 1990.

————. 'Discourse in the Novel.' *The Dialogic Imagination*. Ed. Michael Holquist. Trans. Caryl Emerson and Michael Holquist. Austin: University of Texas Press, 1981.

Benjamin, Walter. *The Origin of the German Tragic Drama*. Trans. John Osborne. London: NLB, 1977.

Bogost, Ian. *Persuasive Games*. Cambridge: MIT Press, 2007.

Bourdieu, Pierre. *The Field of Cultural Production*. Ed. Randal Johnson. New York: Columbia University Press, 1993.

Brown, Bill. 'The Dark Wood of Postmodernity.' PMLA 120.3 (May 2005).

Hammond, Adam. *Literature in the Digital Age*. Cambridge: Cambridge University Press, 2016.

Hansen, Jim. 'Formalism and Its Malcontents: Benjamin and De Man on the Function of Allegory.' *New Literary History* 35.4 (October 2004).

Hudson, Laura. 'Twine, the Video-Game Technology for All.' *New York Times Magazine* (November 19, 2014).

Juul, Jesper. *Handmade Pixels*. Cambridge: MIT Press, 2019.

Larkin, Philip. *All What Jazz*. New York: Farrar, Straus, Giroux, 1970.

Milton, John. *Paradise Lost. The Complete Poems*. Ed. John Leonard. London: Penguin, 1998.

Mouffe, Chantal. *Agonistics*. London: Verso, 2013.

Nietzsche, Friedrich. *The Birth of Tragedy and The Case of Wagner*. Ed. Walter Kaufman. New York: Random House, 1967.

Rancière, Jacques. *The Politics of Aesthetics: The Distribution of the Sensible*. Trans. Gabriel Rockhill. London: Continuum, 2004.

Reynolds, Simon. *Rip It Up and Start Again*. London: Faber and Faber, 2004.

Sarkeesian, Anita and Katherine Cross. 'Your Humanity Is in Another Castle.' *The State of Play*. Eds. Daniel Goldberg and Linus Larsson. New York: Seven Stories Press, 2015.

Shlain, Leonard. *The Alphabet Versus the Goddess*. New York: Viking, 1998.

Superbrothers. 'Less Talk, More Rock.' Boing Boing (March 24, 2010).

Teskey, Gordon. 'Allegory.' *The Spenser Encyclopedia*. Ed. A. C. Hamilton. Toronto: University of Toronto Press, 1990.

Wagner, Richard. *Art and Revolution*. Trans. William Ashton Ellis. London: Kegan Paul, Trench, Trübner & Co, 1895.

Willis, J. H. *Leonard and Virginia Woolf as Publishers: The Hogarth Press, 1917–41* (Charlottesville, VA: University of Virginia Press, 1992).

Woolf, Virginia. 'How It Strikes a Contemporary.' *The Common Reader*. London: Hogarth Press, 1925.

————. 'A Letter to a Young Poet.' *The Hogarth Letters*. London: Hogarth Press, 1932.

————. *A Room of One's Own*. London: Hogarth Press, 1929.

————. *Three Guineas*. London: Hogarth Press, 1938.

Žižek, Slavoj. *The Sublime Object of Ideology*. London: Verso, 1989.

The author thanks:

Craig, for having me along for the ride, the epic chats, and teeing me up so extensively.

Patrick, for inviting me into his home, showing me his favourite spots in Tokyo, and always saying it like it is.

Andy, for tying all my interests together and always having perspective.

Everyone on the JETT Squad who shared their time with me: Sarah Adams, Mack Adams, Sam Bradley, Dustin Harbin, and Randy Smith.

Nick Mount, for starting this ball rolling; Darren Wershler, for the invitation and swanky hotel; Michael Borgstrom, for insisting I teach my dream course; Paul Stevens, for teaching me everything I know about Milton; Melba Cuddy-Keane, for teaching me everything I know about Virginia Woolf; Virginia Woolf, for teaching me how to write.

All my students over the years – particularly the fall 2015 session of CLT 594 at San Diego State University (I told you I would write about that moment, Cheryl!), the Winter 2020 session of BKS 2000 at the University of Toronto, and Edwin Pau and the winter 2018 ENG 287 videogame discussion group.

The *Far Shore* Squad at Coach House: Jason McBride, David Berry, Crystal Sikma, Tali Voron, James Lindsay, and especially Alana Wilcox, for sticking with this project for so many years.

Kieran Drew, for showing me how to beat all the boss battles in *Sworcery*.

Jared Bland, for all kinds of things.

Marta, for everything.

This book is dedicated to the memory of my beloved cat, Wendy, who came into my life at the same time as *Sworcery* and passed out of it just as JETT arrived.

Adam Hammond is Assistant Professor in the Department of English at the University of Toronto. He is the author of *Literature in the Digital Age: A Critical Introduction* (Cambridge University Press, 2016) and co-author of *Modernism: Keywords* (2014). His writing has appeared in *The Walrus, The Literary Review of Canada,* and the *Globe and Mail,* and his work has been profiled in *Wired* and on BBC and CBC radio.

Typeset in Albertina, All Round Gothic, and Graphie.

Printed at the Coach House on bpNichol Lane in Toronto, Ontario, Lynx Cream paper, which was manufactured in Saint-Jérôme, Quebec. This book was printed with vegetable-based ink on a 1973 Heidelberg KORD offset litho press. Its pages were folded on a Baumfolder, gathered by hand, bound on a Sulby Auto-Minabinda, and trimmed on a Polar single-knife cutter.

Coach House is on the traditional territory of many nations including the Mississaugas of the Credit, the Anishnabeg, the Chippewa, the Haudenosaunee, and the Wendat peoples, and is now home to many diverse First Nations, Inuit, and Métis peoples. We acknowledge that Toronto is covered by Treaty 13 with the Mississaugas of the Credit. We are grateful to live and work on this land.

Edited by David Berry
Cover art by Sam Bradley and Craig D. Adams for Superbrothers A/V
Cover and interior design by Crystal Sikma
Author photo by Marta Balcewicz

Coach House Books
80 bpNichol Lane
Toronto ON M5S 3J4
Canada

416 979 2217
800 367 6360

mail@chbooks.com
www.chbooks.com